MA NOTES

including
- *Introduction to the Novel*
- *Brief Synopsis of the Novel*
- *List of Characters*
- *Chapter Summaries and Commentaries*
- *Character Analyses*
- *Flaubert's Life and Works*
- *Questions for Review*

by
James L. Roberts, Ph.D.
Department of English
University of Nebraska

Wiley Publishing, Inc.

About the Author
James L. Roberts, Ph.D., Department of
English, University of Nebraska

Production
Wiley Indianapolis Composition Services

CliffsNotes™ *Madame Bovary*

Published by:
Wiley Publishing, Inc.
111 River Street
Hoboken, NJ 07030
www.wiley.com

Copyright © 1964 Wiley Publishing, Inc., New York, New York

ISBN: 0-8220-0780-0

Printed in the United States of America

14 13 12 11 10

1O/TQ/QZ/QS/IN

Published simultaneously in Canada

CONTENTS

MADAME BOVARY

INTRODUCTION

Gustave Flaubert's masterpiece, *Madame Bovary,* was published in 1857. The book shocked many of its readers and caused a scandalized chain reaction that spread through all France and ultimately resulted in the author's prosecution for immorality.

Since that time, however, *Madame Bovary* has been recognized by students of literature as being the forerunner and model of our most prevalent and influential literary genre, the realistic novel. It is now considered a book of great intrinsic worth and one which contains an important and moving story. In addition, it provides a standard against which to compare the works and writers that have followed it. It is impossible to understand or appreciate modern European and American fiction without an acquaintance with *Madame Bovary.*

A SUMMARY OF *MADAME BOVARY*

Charles Bovary, the only son of a middle-class family, became a doctor and set up his practice in a rural village. He made a marriage of convenience with a woman older than himself. Upon his wife's death, Bovary married an attractive young woman named Emma Rouault, the daughter of one of his patients. For a while Emma was excited and pleased by her marriage, but because of her superficial romantic ideals she was soon bored and disillusioned by her new life. As a result of her dissatisfaction she became ill.

For the sake of her health the Bovarys moved to a new town, where their daughter was born. Emma's unhappiness continued, and she began to have romantic yearnings toward Leon, a young law clerk. After Leon left the town in order to attend law school, Emma's boredom and frustration became more intense. She was negligent of her duties as a wife and mother. None of Bovary's efforts to please her were successful, and she did not value or understand his devoted love for her.

Finally Emma had an adulterous affair with Rodolphe, a local landowner. When he abandoned her, she became seriously ill. After her recovery Emma encountered Leon in Rouen and began to carry on an affair with him. In order to afford weekly trips to the city to see Leon and to satisfy her other whims, Emma spent her husband's money freely and incurred many debts. She kept these secret from Bovary and managed to obtain a Power of Attorney so that she would have full control over their financial affairs.

Eventually her unpaid bills went long overdue and a judgment was obtained against her by her creditors. She owed a vast sum of money, and the sheriff's officers arrived to confiscate the family property. Emma tried frantically to raise the money and finally turned to both Rodolphe and Leon, but neither was willing or able to help. Out of shame and despair, she poisoned herself. Shortly afterwards her husband, now a ruined and broken man, also died, leaving their daughter to a life of poverty.

THE MAIN CHARACTERS

(For a more full analysis of these characters, see section on *Character Analysis*.)

Charles Bovary

A country doctor. He lacks intelligence and imagination; he is naive and unaggressive and has the most conventional and mundane interests.

Emma Bovary

She is portrayed as an irresponsible, immature, and neurotic woman who is unable to adjust to the realities of her life.

Homais

The apothecary at Yonville. He stands for the new middle-class spirit and "progressive" outlook that Flaubert detested so much.

Rodolphe
Emma's first lover, a shrewd bachelor who lives on his estate near Yonville.

Leon
Emma's early friend and later her second lover.

THE SECONDARY CHARACTERS

Marquis d'Andervilliers
A nobleman who invites the Bovarys to a ball at La Vaubyessard, his chateau.

The Blind Beggar
A hideously deformed creature whom Emma encounters several times on the road between Rouen and Yonville, and who passes beneath her window when she is dying. His ugly appearance and ghastly song horrify her whenever they meet. He has been interpreted as a symbol of either Death or the Devil.

Berthe
The daughter of Charles and Emma Bovary.

Binet
The tax collector at Yonville.

Maitre Bocage
Leon's employer at Rouen.

Bournisien
The priest at Yonville. He is a good-natured and simple man but utterly lacking in intelligence, perception, or sophistication. He accepts and defends all the dogmatic and outmoded aspects of official Church thought and never dares to question anything. He has no understanding of the real needs of his parishioners. He represents the ignorance and inadequacies of the rural clergy in Flaubert's time and serves as an effective counterpoint to Homais.

Mme. Bovary the Elder

Charles' mother. In order to compensate for the unhappiness of her marriage, she has been an overly protective and indulgent mother. When her son becomes an adult, she is grasping and domineering and tries to run his life for him. She is jealous of Charles' affection for his wife, and as a result, she and Emma do not get along well.

M. Bovary

Charles' father. He is a former army officer who was forced to resign from the service. He is tyrannical, cruel, and boastful; he spends and drinks too much and is an unfaithful husband.

Canivet

A doctor from a neighboring town who is called in by Bovary after the operation on Hippolyte, during Emma's various illnesses, and at the time of her poisoning. He is hardly more competent than Bovary, but he condescends to him as an inferior, and is smug about his own skill and reputation.

Felicite

Emma's maid.

Maitre Guillaumin

The lawyer at Yonville for whom Leon originally worked. Emma asks him for help near the end of the novel.

Maitre Hareng

A sheriff's officer.

Héloïse

Bovary's first wife.

Hippolyte

The servant at the inn on whom Bovary and Homais unsuccessfully operate.

Hivert

The coachman at Yonville.

Homais

The apothecary at Yonville. He is one of the most successful supporting characters in the novel, because there is a complete identity between his function as a character and his function as the representative of a type. He stands for the new middle-class spirit and "progressive" outlook that Flaubert detested so much. Homais' intellect is limited, and he is poorly educated, but he is pretentious and puffed up with self-esteem. His talk consists of cliches and half-truths, and he demonstrates all the limitations and prejudices of the new bourgeoisie. For example, he is an avowed agnostic and an exponent of Voltaire, yet he is fearful and superstitious in the face of death. Furthermore, he is cowardly and irresponsible, as is shown in the aftermath of the episode concerning the operation on Hippolyte, and though he professes equalitarian principles, he is himself status conscious. Some of the best comic scenes in the novel are the conversations between Homais and his rival, the priest. Flaubert's pessimism is illustrated by the ending of the novel, where Homais' advancement and personal triumph are described.

Mme. Homais

The apothecary's wife; she is a simple and placid woman.

Justin

Homais' teen-age assistant. He is secretly in love with Emma and is seen crying on her grave near the end of the novel. He is naïve and innocent, but ironically it is Justin who is responsible for giving Emma the arsenic.

Lagardy

A well-known tenor whom the Bovarys hear at the opera in Rouen; he is also famed as a lover, and Emma's interest in him serves as an introduction to her meeting with Leon.

Lariviere

A great doctor from Rouen who arrives too late to save Emma's life, and who is consulted on other occasions. He is a brilliant and highly skilled physician and is contemptuous of his less capable colleagues and of such pretentious fools as Homais. He is coldly superior and aloof in his bearing, yet he is the only doctor in the novel to express real sympathy for the suffering of his patients and to show a sense of professional dignity and integrity. Biographers have determined that in this character, Flaubert portrayed his own father.

Mme. Lefrancois
The owner of the inn at Yonville.

Mlle. Lempereur
The teacher in Rouen who is supposedly giving piano lessons to Emma.

Catherine Leroux
An aged peasant woman who is awarded a prize at the Agricultural Show. Her humility and dedication are meant to stand in sharp contrast to Emma's way of life.

Lestiboudois
The general handyman and church sexton at Yonville.

Lheureux
An unscrupulous moneylender and commission merchant at Yonville who entices Emma into debt by playing on her weaknesses and fears. He eventually forces the Bovarys into bankruptcy, thus precipitating Emma's suicide.

Lieuvain
The representative of the Prefect; he makes a speech at the Agricultural Show. His platitudes about patriotism, progress, duty, religion, and the nobility of agriculture serve to illustrate Flaubert's attitude toward the bourgeoisie, and are also an effective counterpoint to the platitudes about love that Rodolphe is whispering to Emma at the same time.

Nastasie
Bovary's first maid; she is fired by Emma after the ball.

Roualt
Emma's father. He is a simple and nearly illiterate peasant, but he is the only character of any significance in the novel who is genuinely warm and unselfish.

Tuvache
 The mayor of Yonville.

Vincart
 A banker who works with Lheureux in his financial transactions.

PART I – CHAPTER 1

Summary
 At the age of fifteen, Charles Bovary struck his schoolmates as a shy and clumsy country lad. He did not have great intelligence or wit but was a diligent and industrious student. He was quiet; however, he mixed well with the other boys.

 His father was a former army surgeon who had been forced to leave the service as a result of some scandal. He was a handsome and unscrupulous man who had married Charles' mother in order to get his hands on her large dowry. After the marriage, he wasted most of the money in foolish speculations, drinking, and amorous affairs. He had always been a cruel and unfaithful husband. In middle age he continued to mistreat his wife and was a bitter, stern, and boastful man. He and his wife eventually acquired and lived on a small farm.

 Charles' mother had once loved her husband deeply, but her unfortunate marriage had cooled this affection and had turned her youthful gaiety and optimism into nervous moodiness and spite.

 After their son's birth, the two Bovarys had often clashed about his rearing, and Charles' boyhood was one of inconsistencies and contradictions. His mother had been overly fond and doting, while his father had attempted to inure him to the rigors of life through austere treatment.

 Eventually Charles was sent to a secondary school and then studied medicine. Although he worked hard at first, his lack of great intelligence and a natural tendency to laziness caused him to fail his examinations. His mother attributed this to unfairness on the part of the examiners, and the news was kept a secret from his father. The following semester, after much hard work, Charles was able to pass. While at the university he had his first real taste of freedom and engaged in several typical student adventures.

After he became a doctor, Charles' mother found him a practice in the village of Tostes, and a wealthy wife in Heloise, an ugly widow who was several years older than he. Charles had hoped that marriage would bring him freedom, but soon found his wife to be as grasping and domineering as his mother had been. Nevertheless, his medical practice prospered.

Comment

A.

Flaubert is presenting in rapid sketches the essential nature and characteristics of some of the background figures, and is preparing us for later actions. For example, it is important to see from the very beginning that Charles is a rather ordinary person with no special talents. He must work exceptionally hard for anything that he achieves. Furthermore, we see that Charles is easily ruled by his mother and later by his wife. He is obedient, diligent, and hard working, but possesses no natural talents.

B.

Flaubert is going to present a novel about the provincial middle-class society. He is interested in this first chapter with presenting a basic picture of the typical country background against which the story takes place.

C.

Note the tremendous contrast between Charles and his father. The father has a dash of charm and imagination that is missing in Charles. The son is more closely aligned with his mother whose main concern is with meeting the bills and getting by in life.

D.

Charles' first marriage is very important in relationship to his later marriage with Emma. First, we see that his wife is able to make him walk a tight line. She is easily able to control him even though she possesses none of the "loveliness" of Emma. She was a real shrew who made life very difficult and unpleasant for Charles. She is so antagonistic that Charles will naturally be more receptive to Emma's charms.

PART I – CHAPTER 2

Summary

Late one night Charles was awakened with a request to come 18 miles out in the country and set a broken leg. He sent the messenger on ahead and promised to follow in a couple of hours. At four in the morning, Charles set out on the journey, trying to search his memory for everything he knew about fractures.

When he arrived at the farm house, he was admitted by a charming young lady. Upon seeing the patient, he was greatly relieved to find a simple fracture with no complications. Mademoiselle Emma came in and assisted with preparing bandages. Charles was struck by the beauty of her flashing brown eyes which appeared to be almost black. When he had finished, she led him into the dining room where he ate and talked with Mademoiselle Emma about the patient. Upon leaving, he promised to come back in three days. But instead, he found himself returning the next day and went twice a week regularly in spite of the long ride. In about eight weeks, the patient was able to walk about.

During the entire episode, Charles never questioned himself as to why he went so often to see the patient, but his wife did. She made inquiries and found out that the patient had a daughter who had been brought up in a convent and was known to give herself airs. After much complaining, nagging, and pleading, Charles' wife finally extracted a promise from him that he would not go there again.

As time passed, Charles' mother and wife both began to pick at him incessantly. Suddenly it was learned that the lawyer who had been administering Heloise's estate had absconded with nearly all her money. Furthermore, it was discovered upon investigation that

14

her remaining property was of little value and that the woman had lied about her wealth prior to the wedding. Bovary's parents had a violent argument about this, and Heloise was very upset. About a week later she had a stroke and died.

Comment

A.

In this chapter, we meet Mademoiselle Emma. But Flaubert is interested in presenting her from a distant view, that is, we hear about her first from other viewpoints. He is saving his personal or direct introduction of Emma until a later chapter and is here presenting Charles' and Heloise's view of Emma. This technique is called the delayed emergence. It functions to arouse the reader's interest in the main character.

B.

It is a part of Charles' character that he is not even aware of why he went so often to see his patient. It might even be said that he was surprised when his wife accused him of going solely to see Mademoiselle Emma. Denied of the privilege of seeing her, Charles determined that he could then justifiably love her at a distance.

C.

Again, note that Charles' present wife is such a shrew, is so bad and so demanding and so ugly ("Her dresses hung on her bony frame."), and is so unpleasant that by contrast Emma seems like an angel to Charles. Thus Charles' miserable experiences with his first wife prepare him to be so indulgent and yielding to Emma later in his life.

D.

The reader who is not aware of Flaubert's method of evoking a scene is missing a large measure of the greatness of this novel. The reader should select a passage, such as Charles' arrival at his patient's house, and examine the careful way in which Flaubert makes you feel this scene. His choice of language and careful description paints an accurate description of what he is writing about. The technique that Flaubert uses may be compared to that of a camera coming slowly in for a close shot and then moving subtly away for another shot.

PART I – CHAPTER 3

Summary

Sometime after, Roualt paid Charles a call to settle his bill and to offer his condolences. He invited Bovary to visit at the farm. Charles accepted the offer and became a frequent guest at the Roualt house. In these circumstances, Bovary's interest in Emma matured, and soon he found himself in love with her.

Emma's father had never been a very good farmer. He had debts and constantly drank the best cider rather than sending it to the market. Thus, when he realized that Charles was interested in Emma, he resolved to give his consent, especially since Emma had never been very good around the farm. Thus Charles' proposal was accepted.

Charles and Emma decided that the wedding would take place as soon as Charles was out of mourning. He visited often and they discussed the details of the wedding. Emma would have preferred a midnight wedding with torches, but her father would not stand for that. Instead, there was a traditional wedding with a party which lasted sixteen hours.

Comment

A.

We should note with what delight Charles observes everything that Emma does. He is charmed with her looks, her way of talking, her actions, and everything about her. He can find no fault with her. This attitude or view toward his future wife will essentially continue during his entire married life, making it easy for Emma to commit her indiscretions.

Charles is infatuated w/ Emma

B.

Flaubert begins already to offer little hints as to Emma's character. We see that her father thinks of her as rather useless around the farm and is not sorry to lose her in marriage. Emma's romanticism, which will later be seen to be the cause of her tragic life, is here suggested by her desire to have a midnight wedding with torches. This is the first hint that Emma is a person who seeks something of the strange and marvelous, something that will break the monotony of living in a dull world.

PART I – CHAPTERS 4 & 5

Summary

The wedding was a gala affair with many friends and relatives present. There was much good fun; the only unpleasant note was the sullen attitude of Bovary's mother who resented not having had a hand in the plans or preparations. Charles' great happiness was apparent to all who saw him, and Emma too seemed pleased by her marriage. After two days at Rouault's farm, the couple returned to Tostes.

Charles proudly led Emma into her new house, the furnishings and arrangement of which are described in great detail. Emma discovered her predecessor's wedding bouquet on display in the bedroom, where Bovary had thoughtlessly left it. She indulged in some morbid thoughts, but her sorrowful mood passed quickly in the excitement of the moment. In the days that followed, Bovary's every thought was with his wife, and all his efforts were devoted to pleasing her. He took her for walks and enjoyed fulfilling her every whim. He had never known that life could be so pleasant. But Emma wondered why she had not attained the happiness she expected from marriage and what happened to such words as "bliss," "passion," and "ecstasy;" words which had sounded so wonderful when read in books.

Comment

A.

Chapter 4 devotes itself to creating a realistic picture of a country wedding. Flaubert, in a few masterful strokes, makes us feel the entire provincial life. Scenes such as these account for Flaubert's title as the first master of perfect realism.

B.

In both chapters, the reader should note how utterly Charles dotes on Emma. His dogged devotion accounts for his later blindness to Emma's faults and his later desire to fulfill her every whim.

C.

Emma's desire to change the house should not be seen as a touch of individuality on her part. Rather, she will be seen to be constantly desiring a change, thinking that in every change she will find the happiness that she is seeking.

D.

The first blow to Emma's romantic nature comes when she sees the still preserved bridal bouquet held over from Charles' first marriage. This takes away from the sentimentality she is trying to attach to her own bouquet.

E.

At the end of Chapter 5, Emma's true nature is beginning to emerge. She is already disillusioned because marriage is not as great in real life as it was in her books. She is disappointed because she has not found all of the "bliss, passion, and ecstasy" that she had read about in novels. This idea will now be developed as the main theme of the book. That is, the contrast Emma finds between the realistic world and her dreams of what life should be.

PART I – CHAPTER 6

Summary

Emma recalls her thirteenth year, when her father took her to the convent to live. She enjoyed the convent at first; she liked talking with the nuns and she enjoyed answering the difficult questions correctly. But she soon relinquished herself to the languid atmosphere of the convent and found herself admiring the beauty of the chapel rather than listening to the lessons. She gave herself over to romantic notions concerning the church and dreamed of the "sick lamb" and the metaphors of a "betrothed spouse, heavenly lover, marriage everlasting," and she listened only to the romantic melancholy of the lamentations.

There was an old maid who came to the convent and who would sing romantic ballads to the girls on the sly. Emma then read voraciously from tales of romance involving lonely meetings, secret encounters, gloomy forests, and troubles of the heart. She became enthusiastic over Sir Walter Scott and dreamed of living in some romantic palace where a cavalier with a white plume could come galloping up and rescue her.

When her mother died, Emma had a lock of her dead mother's hair mounted and wrote her father that when she died she would like to be buried in the same grave. She gave her time to reading romantic, sentimental poetry and while enjoying the mysteries of the church, she rebelled against the discipline.

When her father took her from the convent, she enjoyed managing the servants for a while, but soon tired of it and longed for the convent. When Charles appeared, she found it difficult to believe that the quietness and dullness of her romance was what she had read about in the novels.

Comment

A.

The earliest chapters have been concerned with Emma only from an indirect view. Now Flaubert is ready to present his view or analysis of Emma. As pointed out earlier, this technique — a delayed emergence of the main character — serves to heighten the reader's interest in hearing about the main character.

B.

This chapter presents Emma as an incurable romantic, a person who lives in a dream world, in a world of fiction rather than in the real world. She is a dreamer and a sentimentalist. When young she had read *Paul and Virginia,* a highly sentimental and romanticized view of life and love. This novel of idyllic love contributed to Emma's dreamy sentimentalism. The chapter then proceeds to show how a person already endowed with a strong degree of sentimentality was placed in a type of life in the convent which nourished her already excessive tendency toward this type of sentimentalism. In religion she searched for the unusual, the mystic, the dreamy. In the convent, she read stories of romance while being unable to see the real world. She concentrated her attention upon the beautiful and artistic rather than finding the basic elements of a natural life. Novels read on the sly only increased the value of the romance by being forbidden. Thus, left alone with her dreams, she developed into a dreamy girl who wanted all the elements of romantic fiction to come alive in her own life. She longs for old castles, for romantic lovers charging up to a balcony on a white horse, for moonlight meetings in far-away places. She feels the need of excitement and mystery, and cannot tolerate the normal life of everyday living. Thus, when Charles comes calling, she cannot understand why her life wasn't suddenly filled with passion, bliss and ecstasy.

C.

Another of Emma's characteristics is suggested in this chapter: Emma's constant need for a change. She at first enjoyed being out of the convent and at home managing the servants, but then grew rapidly tired of this and longed again for the convent. Thus throughout the novel, Emma will begin one project and drop it only to begin another, always in the constant search for something new and exciting.

PART I—CHAPTER 7

Summary

Emma wondered if the honeymoon was actually to be the finest part of her life. She wondered why she couldn't be standing in a Swiss chalet with a husband in a dashing outfit of velvet, soft boots, peaked hat, etc. As Charles' outward attraction for her increased, she began inwardly to detach herself from him. As she observed Charles, she noted that he simply trudged through every day. His talk was dull, he provoked no emotions in her, he had no desire to do or see anything, and he couldn't even explain a riding term in one of her novels. Ideally, she dreamed of a man who would introduce her into a multitude of activities and passions, who would inspire her to live to the fullest. And when she perceived that Charles was perfectly content simply to be with her, she hated him for his placid immobility and contentment.

Charles, on the other hand, found no fault with his wife. She was an excellent manager and played the piano with skill. All her acts gave him pleasure, and in every way he was content with his life and good fortune. Whenever Mrs. Bovary visited, however, he was confounded by the coldness between his wife and mother. Emma resented the older woman's advice or interference, and the mother was jealous of her son's affection for his wife.

Meanwhile, Emma continued to crave the exalted and passionate love which she sadly felt had been denied her. She criticized herself for ever having married and suffered from envy of the imagined happiness of the girls with whom she had gone to school.

One September the Bovarys were invited to a ball at the chateau of the Marquis d'Andervilliers, whom Charles had treated. The Marquis was far above them in social rank but wanted to demonstrate his gratitude for the service Bovary had done him. Emma looked forward to this unique event with great eagerness.

Comment

A.

Emma continues her dreaming of another life and another husband. She pictures to herself a fabulous life with another person, and begins to detach herself from Charles. The contrast between her dreams and her life is brought out rather concisely in two paragraphs, the first describing Charles' commonplace banalities, his slow plodding ways, his lack of emotional stimulation and his contentment, whereas in her dreams, she sees a man sweeping her off her feet and introducing her to all the intense passions of life. Finally, to observe her dull husband being content with a snack, falling into bed, and snoring fills her with indescribable longings for another life.

B.

This chapter then begins to depict the complete contrast between Emma and Charles. His plodding nature and his routine ardors and embraces destroyed all the excitement in life for Emma. She becomes increasingly irritated with his coarse ways and his dullness. This chapter then marks the beginning of her life of waiting for something exciting to happen. Her entire life will be characterized by her unfilled longing and incessant waiting for some excitement to enter into it. Her disappointment prompted her first words to be spoken in the novel: "O God, O God, why did I get married?"— previous to this statement, we have heard about Emma and about her thoughts, but significantly, these are her *first* spoken words.

C.

The excitement that Emma has been waiting for comes in the form of an invitation to La Vaubyessard. This will soon become one of the high points of her life.

PART I – CHAPTER 8

Summary

The chateau was a building of stately proportions, situated on a large and prosperous estate. The many rooms were filled with expensive and artistic furnishings and decorations. The ball was attended by all the aristocracy and gentry of the surrounding area.

Emma was overjoyed at the opportunity of being able to move freely in such noble company. During their stay at the chateau she constantly berated Bovary, whom she felt looked like a country buffoon and whose presence embarrassed her. Emma dressed and attempted to behave as if she too were a great lady and mingled with the other guests. All night she basked in the reflected glory of those around her. The ball and the people at it seemed to be transported from out of the novels and dreams she had long cherished. Emma was so ecstatic she never noticed that most of the guests ignored her. The high point of her evening came when a man known only as "Vicomte" danced with her.

On the trip home Emma suffered from bitter disappointment that she, who was so obviously entitled to preferment, could not live this way all year round. In her disillusionment she saw Bovary as a clumsy, simple oaf. Back home her frustration caused her to be cross with him, and in a fit of pique she fired the maid, despite the woman's devotion and good service. Each day Emma attempted to recall the great events of the ball, but in time they became vague memories.

Comment

A.

This chapter presents in reality all of the grand elegance that Emma had dreamed and read about. Here then are her dreams turning into reality. Everything that she dreamed of is here: the grand dinner, the magnificent ball, the elegant dances, the discussions of far away people and even an old man who had slept with the queen, and a young lady carrying on an intrigue with a young man. And finally, Emma's being requested to dance with a Viscount testifies to her own superiority over her upbringing.

B.

This chapter focuses almost all of the attention on Emma. It is important here to see that Emma *does* possess the necessary qualities so as to blend in with an aristocratic world. Unlike Charles who stands limply around for five hours watching a game he doesn't understand, Emma is moving graciously and rather charmingly amid this aristocratic society. Even though she does not attract people to her, she seems to blend in. Her invitation to dance with the Viscount and her ability to learn the dance attest to her acceptance. Thus, Emma's later degradation should be contrasted to the success she attains here, and by the comparison, Emma's later plight will be seen to be more pathetic.

C.

Note the cigar box that Charles found. Emma will later dawdle over this as a reminder of her experience at the ball and convince herself that it belonged to the Viscount.

D.

Returning to her own drab surroundings, Emma can barely tolerate the dull routine of everyone doing the same dull things. She therefore loses herself in her reveries about the ball.

PART I – CHAPTER 9

Summary

Emma buried herself in her fantasies and dreamed of living in Paris, among the nobility. She visualized life in the capital as a constant round of balls, parties, amours, and other exciting things. She read novels and travel books voraciously and studied maps of the city. Much of her time was spent planning imaginary trips, adventures, secret meetings, and visits to the theater or opera. The reality of life at Tostes became unbearable to her, and she was even more critical of Bovary.

At first Emma attempted to add little touches of elegance to her humdrum life, such as fancy lampshades and silver, but this soon became an unsatisfactory solution to her craving, even though it pleased Charles. Emma's despair became more intense when she finally was forced to realize that there would be no further invitations to the chateau, and in her depression she gave up her music, sketching, and other pursuits. She was often sad and lonely, and during the long winter her plight became worse. She seemed to cultivate her unhappiness and self-pity by concentrating on her unattainable aspirations, and by finding so little with which to occupy herself. Most of her time was now spent staring down from her window at the village street. She was sullen and rarely spoke to Charles.

As her condition became even worse, Emma's moods began to fluctuate between extreme forms of behavior. Sometimes she was very active, sometimes lethargic and slovenly, sometimes nervous and stingy, sometimes capricious and temperamental, but always she was unpredictable and difficult to get along with. Soon she became physically ill. None of Charles' worried efforts to cure her were successful, and he took her to Rouen, to see the medical professor under whom he had studied.

This learned doctor recommended a change of scene for the sake of Emma's health, since it was evidently a nervous disorder and she complained so much of disliking Tostes. Despite the fact that he had built a flourishing practice in the village, Charles was willing to sacrifice all for Emma's welfare. After making some inquiries, he decided to move to the town of Yonville, which was located in a nice area and where a doctor was needed.

While Emma was helping with the packing, she pricked her hand on her old bridal bouquet, which was now dried up, frayed and yellow with dust. She threw it into the fire and watched it burn. By the time they moved to the new town, Emma was pregnant.

Comment

A.

Perhaps no chapter in the novel presents Flaubert's essential theme and meaning as well as does this concluding chapter of Part One. Flaubert vividly depicts the exhausting and enervating results of a woman who expends all her energy in dreams and futile longings. The chapter opens with Emma's recalling the events of the ball, reliving certain episodes and then progressing to envisioning new incidents which might have happened. She wastes, then, her energies in imagining that the cigar case belonged to the Viscount, that he is now in Paris and is pursuing a life of intrigue and excitement. She fritters away her time and energy by tracing walks through Paris on a map she bought, she imagines shopping in Paris, she subscribes to Paris magazines and she dreams of the Viscount. But Flaubert is able to make us all see that Emma's frustrated longing for a different type of life is a quality that we all possess. Thus he universalizes Emma's longings so as to make an indirect comment concerning this type of wasted and futile activity.

B.

Emma constantly contrasts her real environment and surroundings with those she conjectures in her dreams. The real then seems completely intolerable: "The nearer home things came, the more she shrank from all thought of them." In her dreams, new and exciting things happen every day, but in her real life in Tostes, the same things happen over and over again, so that "the whole of her immediate environment — dull countryside, imbecile petty bourgeois, life in its ordinariness — seemed a freak, a particular piece of bad luck that had seized on her." Therefore, she tries to introduce some elegance into her life; she hires a fourteen-year-old girl and tries to teach her how to become a "lady's maid."

C.

Emma's frustration and longings cause her to give up her piano, her needle work, drawing, care for the house and all other useful activity. Instead, she fritters away her time in daydreaming. Rather than making herself useful in some way, she drains herself of all her energy by these longings for another life. In waiting for something to happen, she becomes a pathetic (almost tragic) case of a woman who exhausts herself in these futile longings until she is physically sick. In other words, she indulges in her own misery until her self-indulgences cause her sickness. She has had a fleeting glimpse at emotions that transcend the dull routine life at Tostes, and her intense longings for these more sublime emotions cause her sickness. The pathos of Emma's life is that she does possess enough sensitivity to be aware of feelings and emotions greater than those of Charles, but is unable to find a suitable outlet for these emotions.

D.
   Emma's plight is symbolically depicted in the discovery and burning of her bridal bouquet. What was once to be the symbol of a new and exciting life filled with new emotions now is seen as a faded, frayed, dusty object on which she pricks her finger. Thus, the burning of the bridal bouquet signifies the end of her marriage and prepares us for her promiscuity later on. It is not just the end of a marriage, but also the end of her life at Tostes, because now that they are moving, Emma can perhaps be reawakened to a different life.

PART II – CHAPTERS 1 & 2

Summary
   Yonville was a market town located in the center of a farming district, not far from Rouen. The main features of the surrounding region and of the town itself are described in some detail. Various inhabitants of Yonville, including Madame Lefrancois, the innkeeper, Hivert and Artemise, her servants, Binet, the tax collector, and Homais, the apothecary, make their first appearances in this chapter.

   Homais, with whom Bovary had corresponded before deciding to move to Yonville, was an outspoken and pretentious fellow of some education and status. He was always eager to impress people by his knowledge and sophistication, although in fact he did not possess much of either.

The Bovarys and Felicite, their new maid, arrived in Yonville after a very tiring trip and an accident in which Emma lost her pet greyhound. She was in her usual irritable mood.

Bovary and his wife dined at the inn. They were joined at the table by Homais and his boarder, Leon, a shy young man who was the town lawyer's clerk. During the meal Homais devoted most of his attention to Bovary, seeking to awe him by his extensive acquaintance with science and local affairs. Meanwhile, Emma and Leon fell into conversation. He shared many of her romanticized notions and was also an avid reader of sentimental novels. An immediate rapport sprang up between them. Their talk consisted of platitudes and conventionalities, but they each interpreted them as sensitive and profound observations.

Later on the Bovarys took possession of their new house. Emma recalled the other places in which she had lived and been unhappy. She hoped that the future would bring an improvement in her life.

Comment

A.

Flaubert's masterful description and rendition of the town is a masterpiece of realistic writing. It captures all of the mediocrity of a small town. And what Flaubert never says directly, but depicts through his descriptions is that this town is just about the same as was Tostes. Yonville is just as monotonous, routine, and boring as was Tostes. Here, nothing has changed in years and nothing will change. So suddenly, we realize that this town will depress Emma as much as did Tostes.

B.

We meet the chemist Homais for the first time. He will develop into a stereotype. It will suffice here to begin to note certain characteristics which make up the stereotype. 1) He is the man who professes to keep up with the times. 2) He feels it is his duty to ridicule the church, therefore aligning himself with the advanced thinkers of the world. 3) He has accumulated many facts which he enjoys reciting, but the reader should note that his facts are of a trivial nature.

C.

Emma's first meeting with Leon is an exciting event for her. For the first time in her life, she has met a person who shares the same interest in literature, music, and related subjects. She immediately feels that they are kindred spirits and an immediate rapport sprang up between them. But the reader should note that their talk consisted of platitudes and conventionalities, but they each interpreted them as sensitive and profound observations.

PART II—CHAPTER 3

Summary

All the next day Leon thought about Emma, for their meeting had been a very special event to him. This was the first time that the bashful youth had ever spoken to a lady at such length, and he was surprised at his own eloquence.

In the days that followed, Homais was of great assistance to Bovary in establishing himself, although it must be said that the druggist's motives were partly selfish. Charles was a bit gloomy, because his medical practice was slow in starting and he had financial worries. The cost of moving had been high, he had lost money on the sale of the house at Tostes, and there was now a child on the way. However, the thought of having a baby Emma to love also, and to watch grow, was a source of great joy to him.

Emma had originally been surprised by her pregnancy but was now accustomed to the idea. She was eager to have the child, although all the preparations made her impatient since they could not afford the kind of layette she insisted was necessary. She hoped the baby would be a boy, for she felt that only a man could have the freedom and strength to overcome the constraints that had always so frustrated her.

The child was born, and after much discussion the name of

"Berthe" was selected. There was a gay christening party, and Bovary's parents visited at Yonville for a month.

One day Emma decided to visit the baby at the home of its wet nurse. She was still weak after her confinement and was beginning to feel faint, when she encountered Leon. She asked him to accompany her. Leon consented and by nightfall, rumors had spread through the town that Madame Bovary was compromising herself.

After seeing the child, Madame Bovary was pestered with lots of trivial requests from the nurse. She quickly consented to give the woman more supplies and even some brandy for the woman's husband. Then she and Leon took a long stroll along the river. Even though they didn't say very much to each other, both were aware of a strange bliss and a deeper communication. After Leon left her, he thought how radiantly she stood out, especially amid all the banalities of Yonville.

Comment

A.

When Emma first learned she was pregnant, she thought that this could be a new experience for her, could fill her empty life with excitement, especially if it were a boy. But when the girl was born, she soon lost interest in it. Again this shows Emma's erratic nature, her inability to maintain an interest in any aspect of life. Her reaction differs significantly with Charles' and the difference emphasizes the growing breach between them. Charles thinks that with the birth of the child, he will have been through the entire range of human experience.

B.

Emma's indiscretion in asking Leon to accompany her, foreshadows her later promiscuities. We have seen that Emma possesses an impetuous nature, and this quality will also contribute to her series of indiscretions.

C.

Emma's encounter with the nurse foreshadows her handlings with the various tradesmen which will later take her so deeply in debt. It seems that Emma would rather give in than discuss the needs of the nurse. Later, her financial troubles are a result of her impetuousness and her failure to consider her needs.

PART II – CHAPTERS 4 & 5

Summary
During the winter Emma's favorite pursuit was to sit at the window and watch the street. She often saw Leon as he passed and had a new and unknown feeling at those moments.

Homais lived across the street and was a frequent caller, especially at mealtimes. He enjoyed gossiping about Bovary's patients and discussing science, philosophy, and politics with the doctor. It was the druggist who always did most of the talking.

On Sundays the Bovarys usually visited the Homais family. Leon was always there, and a bond rapidly developed between him and Emma. They used to sit together and discuss fashions or books while the others played cards or dozed.

Leon began to grow confused and was tormented by these meetings. He was uncertain whether Emma responded to his feelings for her. He was afraid to displease her by remaining silent about his love, but he did not have the courage to declare himself.

One Sunday in February, Homais and his children, the Bovarys, and Leon went on an outdoor excursion. Emma watched the men with interest and decided that she was disgusted by Charles' commonplace appearance and personality.

That night she suddenly realized that Leon loved her. This novel idea pleased her, and she began to complain to herself about the cruel fate which had separated the two of them. Later that week Leon paid her a visit, on some weak pretext. They were both shy and their conversation was stilted, for they feared to express their real feelings to each other.

As time passed Emma began to lose weight through worry. She found a delicious pleasure in contemplating her affection for Leon and contrasting it with her sensible, though unsatisfying role of the virtuous wife. She was herself as a martyr to marital fidelity. Emma became irritable again and was exasperated by Bovary's placid ignorance of her torments. She blamed him for all her troubles and in addition was overly tolerant in judging herself and her behavior. She dreamed of running away with Leon but then doubted his love for her. She wished that Bovary were a cruel husband so that she would have an excuse to be unfaithful. Her nervousness and tension often caused her to engage in fits of weeping.

One day while she was dreaming of Leon, Monsieur Lheureux, a draper, paid her a visit in order to show her some of his wares, especially scarves and little ornaments. He then slyly let her know that he was also a moneylender in case she ever needed to borrow a little money.

As Emma came to the realization of her love for Leon, she tried to compensate for her frustrated love by being the ideal wife, mother and housekeeper. But while she was being the model wife, "she was all desire and rage and hatred."

Comment

A.

In these chapters, Flaubert is developing the love between Emma and Leon, a love that will not be consummated until the third part of the novel. Emma's love causes her to despise her husband, then she turns into the model wife trying to compensate for her lack of love, and finally turns to moods of despair. This again emphasizes Emma's lack of stability and her constant fluctuation between opposite extremes. These moods foreshadow her later sickness and ultimately her suicide.

B.

Monsieur Lheureux is here introduced. He is the money-lender who will unscrupulously play on Emma's weaknesses and will be the cause of her suicide. His portrayal here already suggests his obsequious personality.

PART II – CHAPTER 6

Summary
One evening the tolling of church bells made Emma recall her childhood and school days. She mused about the solace she had often found then through religious devotions and set out for the church, hoping that there she might resolve her present problems and gain some inner peace.

She met the curé, Abbe Bournisien, near the entrance, where he was attempting to control the mischievous children of his catechism class. Emma attempted to explain to the priest her need for spiritual help, but the priest's attention focused more on the young boys who were misbehaving. He was also more interested in telling Emma about his problems within the parish than he was in listening to her. After several attempts on Emma's part to explain her dilemma, she finally sighed in despair: "O God, O God!" The Abbe immediately thinks she has some physical ailment, and advises her to go home immediately and have a cup of tea. Then "it suddenly struck him: 'there was something you were asking me. What was it, now? I can't recall.'" Emma responds that it was nothing and then leaves as the Abbe goes in to teach catechism to the group of boys.

She continued to be very jumpy and tense. That same evening, in a fit of nervous annoyance, she pushed the baby away from her. Berthe fell and cut herself. Emma screamed for help and claimed that the child had been hurt accidentally while playing. After some confused excitement, Bovary and Homais (who always appeared whenever anything of interest happened) managed to calm her and take care of Berthe.

Leon found that his position in Yonville remained perplexing and intolerable. He adored Emma, but saw no future in his love for a married woman. He decided to go to Paris to study law, something he had long spoken of doing. The idea of being alone in the capital frightened him, but he saw no other alternative. After a while though, he began to imagine with great joy the Bohemian adventures he would have there.

Leon made his arrangements and the day finally came for his departure. When he bid farewell to Emma, they were both restrained and shy, although their eyes and gestures communicated a wealth of emotional meanings. After he had gone, Homais and Bovary discussed the dangers and temptations of life in the city. Emma listened silently.

Comment

A.

When Emma thinks of the consolation she had at the convent, she fails to remember that she was also terribly dissatisfied there. Emma is actually looking for some experience that will fill her void and occupy her so that she will not think about her misery. In other words, she is using religion as a substitute for real experiences and as a way of forgetting her present misery.

B.

In this brief scene between Emma and the priest, Flaubert offers a masterful condemnation of the church in a very subtle way. The priest is so occupied with his own insignificant occupation that he does not have time to perceive Emma's distress. In fact, he thinks that she needs a cup of tea rather than spiritual guidance. His devout devotion to details renders him incapable of recognizing Emma's spiritual need and thus he fails in his greater mission as a Priest.

C.

This chapter presents the departure of Leon without a physical consummation of their love. But the length of this mutual attraction and Emma's many reflections about it make her more receptive for her next encounter. In other words, she regrets her timidity in not letting Leon know of her love so that now she is emotionally prepared to respond more openly to the advances of Rodolphe. It can also be said that both Emma and Leon have progressed in their education so that when they next meet, they will not be so bashful and timid.

PART II – CHAPTER 7

Summary

After Leon had gone, Emma began a period of secret mourning. She drifted about aimlessly and was often melancholy. She saw Leon in her imagination as the hero of all her dreams and remembered their walks and conversations. She reproached herself for not having responded to his love, and he became the center of all her thoughts. In her misery, she began again the strange and unpredictable behavior that had marked her in Tostes. Her moods constantly changed, and she was often giddy and nervous.

One day Rodolphe Boulanger, a handsome and wealthy landowner, brought one of his servants to be treated by Bovary. While there he saw Emma and was immediately attracted by her good looks and ladylike bearing. Boulanger was a suave bachelor, both coarse and shrewd. At once his thoughts turned to Emma's seduction, and he began to lay his plans.

Comment

A.

Emma's long melancholy and regret over not having seized her opportunity with Leon actually caused her to become sick. She then goes into one of her spending sprees, justifying her spending by feeling she has sacrificed so much by being faithful to Charles. These are the same types of spending sprees which will later lead her into heavy debts.

B.

Note again Emma's erratic actions. She would take something up, leave it, go to something else only to leave it, etc. It seems that nothing fulfills her. Flaubert's description of Emma's actions and looks implies that Emma fits ironically into the tradition of the courtly love. The "vaporish airs," the fact that she was "pale all over, white as a sheet," and given to spells of dizziness are all characteristics of the courtly love tradition or are signs of disappointed or unfulfilled love.

C.

X

Emma is, after all, essentially middle-class, but she is also more than this. In a sense, she raises herself above the town because unlike others, she is vaguely aware that there are emotions of a higher and purer nature than those with which she finds herself surrounded. This realization does raise Emma in our estimates although this is also the ultimate cause of her tragedy.

D.

Note that Rodolphe is able to see through Emma immediately. He sees her boredom, recognizes that she dislikes her husband and her present life, and realizes that she is "gasping for love" and is ready for a love affair. What we know is that this is true, but partly because she regrets not having an affair with Leon.

PART II CHAPTER 8

Summary

At the time of this story, the annual Agricultural Show for the Prefecture of the Seine-Inferieure was held at Yonville. Everyone looked forward to the fair with great enthusiasm; when the long awaited day finally arrived, Yonville was crowded with visitors from all the surrounding farms and towns. There were exhibits and contests of many kinds, and everything had a carnival aspect. The most important event of the day was the speech and presentation of awards by a representative of the Prefect.

According to his carefully calculated plan, Rodolphe took advantage of the excitement of the day to renew his acquaintance with Emma. They went walking together and spoke about a variety of things. Rodolphe took every opportunity to drop some hint about his love for Emma. He gradually leads her toward the city hall so that they can be alone.

Meanwhile the representative from the Prefect arrived, and even though the people expected the Prefect himself, they were still honored by this man. However, in trying to pay homage to him, the battalion of men confused their orders and everything ended in confusion. While he spoke about the government, Rodolphe begins to hint to Emma his affections for her. And while the speech is going on in the background about the morality and government, Rodolphe begins to declare his love for Emma and to insist that his feelings are nobler than common morality. He continues to declare his love for her in high sounding language while the representative of the Prefect awards prizes to various people.

After the awarding of the prices, Emma separates from Rodolphe and does not see him again until that night at the banquet and later at the fireworks. She was complimented by his attentions, but had constantly acted as she thought proper for a respectable, married woman. As the fireworks were being set off, Emma watched Rodolphe. She was not even aware that the fireworks had gotten wet and wouldn't go off. Later, however, Homais wrote a glowing account of the entire day's activities.

Comment

A.

The inexperienced reader will often overlook the greatness of this particular chapter. It is often referred to when the subject of Flaubert's greatness is being discussed. It will profit the reader to re-read the chapter and observe many of the following factors: the number of things that are contrasted; the use of subtle irony, especially in passages that seem to be simply description; the elaborately described show, the gold medal won by the old peasant woman, and the subtle but damning description of the pompous dignitaries; and the use of foreshadowing, especially in the way in which Emma is able to see unknowingly her whole pathetic life unfold before her in symbolic events.

B.

Use of Contrast and Description: There are so many masterfully descriptive passages, it will suffice to point out only one. In the first part of the chapter, Flaubert is describing all the animals that are gathered together for the show. Most of the details of this description suggest symbolically that this animal world is the same world in which the action of the entire novel is being played.

The animals are described in the same manner in which people will later be described. For example, later in the chapter, when Flaubert is describing the feast, the same type of description is used for both the animals and the people. They were both herded into a small place with noses together, sweating and stuffing themselves. One could even maintain that the animals are described in terms of people and the people are described in terms of animals, emphasizing the nature of the people that Flaubert is dealing with.

C.

   Use of Irony: The speech of the representative of the Prefect is filled with cliches and pompous platitudes. The speaker says only what every other speaker has been saying for years, but yet his speech is highly praised.

   Rodolphe's speech to Emma, delivered against the background of the general prizes being awarded, is a masterpiece of irony. First, we hear about the old peasant woman who is winning a prize for fifty-four years of faithful service and fidelity as a servant. At the same time, Emma is planning on being unfaithful and on beginning a love affair with Rodolphe whom we know can never be faithful to any person very long.

   It is a further stroke of irony that his false speeches of passion such as "I stayed with you, because I couldn't tear myself away..." are spoken during the awarding of the first prize in *manure*. Subtly speaking, Rodolphe's speech is just so much manure, but Emma is not capable of recognizing it.

D.

   Foreshadowing: In the discussion of Lheureux's being the cause of the downfall of a certain man, we are warned that Emma will herself get into trouble because of her dealings with this man. He is even described here as a wheedling, grovelling creature.

   The tremendous waste of human energy in preparing for the show indicates how the energies of Emma are wasted throughout the entire novel.

Emma's view of the ancient *Hirondelle* as it approaches the town, foreshadows her degradation and involvement with Leon later in the novel, as this coach will be instrumental in her love affair.

E.

Homais' role in the entire pageant and his essay sent to the paper afterwards reaches the height of the comic absurd. First of all, from all of the description, the entire day was a failure if not a fiasco. The dignitary was late and when he finally arrived he was only a representative of the Prefect; the presentation of arms was sloppy, confused, and ridiculous; the speeches were dull; there were not enough seats; the feast was long and noisy and badly served and too crowded; the fireworks were damp and would not go off, and it rained during the proceedings. But Homais' account of the day written for the newspaper was so frankly false that his exaggerations seem the height of the comic. And ironically speaking, an earlier description of Homais' says that he "had the right form of words for every conceivable occasion."

PART II—CHAPTERS 9 & 10

Summary

During the next six weeks Rodolphe did not see Emma. This interval was also planned by him, acting on the theory that "absence makes the heart grow fonder." He had carefully analyzed her personality and decided to take advantage of all her frustrations and weaknesses.

When Rodolphe finally called at the Bovary house, Emma, who had thought about him often and was insulted by his lack of attention, was unresponsive. But Rodolphe was so eloquent in amorous language that she soon forgot her affected annoyance at his absence and was overcome by sentiment. When Charles came in, Rodolphe suggested that perhaps riding would be good for Emma. He offered to lend them a horse, but Emma refused. After Rodolphe had gone, Charles convinced Emma to accept Rodolphe's offer and even wrote to Rodolphe himself requesting the horse.

The next day Emma and Rodolphe went for a ride together. He led her to a beautiful and deserted glade in the nearby forest. When they had dismounted, Rodolphe again spoke of his passion for her. Emma was frightened by his intensity but quickly forgot all her good intentions and gave herself entirely to him. When she returned home that night she was radiant with joy. In her new happiness she identified herself with all the daring and romantic heroines of literature whom she had always envied and admired. She unbelievingly repeated to herself over and over again, "I have a lover—a lover."

From this day on the affair between Emma and Rodolphe progressed with great speed. They frequently exchanged love letters and had many secret meetings. Rodolphe was always in Emma's thoughts. She often slipped from her house in the early morning while Bovary was still asleep in order to surprise Rodolphe and have a few extra hours with him.

After a while, Rodolphe, who was a practical and realistic man, became concerned about Emma's imprudent behavior. He spoke to her about this, claiming to be worried lest she compromise herself, and soon she too became nervous. She began to be troubled by feelings of guilt. The pair took precautions to keep their correspondence hidden and worked out an arrangement so that Rodolphe could meet Emma at night in her garden or even in her house, once Bovary had fallen into his usual deep sleep. Rodolphe began to visit her several times each week.

He was sometimes troubled by her wildly romantic fancies and feared that she would do something irrational or impractical, in accord with her silly ideas. He thought of ending their relationship but procrastinated because of the great physical appeal she had for him. So far as Emma's love for him was concerned, Rodolphe cynically doubted her sincerity and had no compunctions about using or abandoning her. Emma, on the other hand, considered him the one great love for whom she had always yearned and surrendered herself to him with complete devotion.

As time passed, Emma became unhappy about both her marriage and adultery. She was often negligent of her duties and then, in a moment of guilty realization, would engage in a brief spurt of activity or maternal affection. Her guilt kept bothering her, and for a short period she even decided to repent and reform. She derived a strange pleasure from her masochistic decision to assuage her guilt through self-sacrifice, for her affection for Rodolphe had not lessened. In order to end the affair, she was cold to him and she planned to force herself to love and assist Bovary.

Comment

A.

Emma is a woman of romantic longings. We saw earlier that she longed for a man who "should know about everything; excel in a multitude of activity, introduce you to passion in all its force, to life in all its graces, you into all mysteries," (see Chapters 6 and 7 of Part I), and now Rodolphe comes to call after a six week's absence, and tells her things she "had never been told before." Here then is the romantic dream come true. *But,* in reality, he is not the knight in shining armor. He is, after all, a thirty-four year old farmer. But to Emma who has lived in boredom so long and who has longed for some type of escape, he is the fulfillment of her dreams. After she surrenders to him, she then thinks of all the heroines of books and compares her shoddy seduction in the woods to those of the romanticized heroines of her novels. She is convinced that her affair has all the "passion, ecstasy and delirium" of the fictionalized accounts in romances. Emma then attempts to make her shoddy affair conform to those of fictionalized accounts. She insists that they leave letters for each other in secret hiding places. She comforts him about absurd insignificant events and when once she thinks she hears Charles coming, she expects Rodolphe to grab his pistol so as to defend himself. She insists upon exchanging miniatures, locks of hair, and even rings. Even Rodolphe realizes the degree of sentimentality that Emma is attaching to their love affair.

B.

Emma never realizes that Rodolphe is simply using her for a pretty mistress. Even though they are having their affair now in Charles' consulting room, she fails to realize how shoddy the affair is and continues to force their affair into the pattern of a great love.

C.

Ironically, it was Charles who originally assured the success of the love affair by insisting that Emma accept Rodolphe's offer of the riding horse. Of course, we have seen earlier that Charles, due to the horror of his first wife, can see no fault in Emma.

D.

Chapter 9 ends with Rodolphe's admonition to Emma that she is compromising herself by her visits to his cabin. This foreshadows his rejection of Emma. We know from the beginning that this is to be only a brief love affair for him, but as he reminds her of her position, we note already that he is beginning to tire of her.

PART II – CHAPTER 11

Summary

One day it was learned that a doctor in Rouen had published a remarkable new surgical procedure for curing clubfoot. Emma and Homais urged Charles to carry out the new operation on Hippolyte, the crippled servant at the inn. Emma hoped in this way to advance Bovary in his career and thus satisfy her desire to be a good wife; she had many daydreams about the wealth and increased prestige to which his success would entitle them. Homais expected to gain personal repute from his own part in the operation and to bring more business to Yonville (and himself) as word of the cure spread. Neither Homais nor Emma was particularly concerned with the safety of the operation or the well-being of Hippolyte.

Bovary was dubious about the new technique and was unwilling to cooperate, but, under the combined pressure of Emma and Homais, finally gave in. Moreover, nearly everyone in the town, including the mayor, was a staunch advocate of the new operation, for they had all been convinced by Homais of its advantage to them. Their ceaseless prodding continued until Bovary was ready to proceed. Hippolyte was terrified and confused by the whole idea, but he was a simple youth and was induced to volunteer his body for the sake of Yonville and Science.

The operation was carried out by Homais and Charles in the local inn. At first it seemed a success, but Hippolyte soon became ill and suffered terrible pain. It was discovered that his leg was infested with gangrene. Bovary was very upset and unable to act; so a consultant was called in from another town. The doctor sternly admonished Bovary for his foolish treatment and amputated the patient's leg. Homais, meanwhile, disclaimed any responsibility, and Emma was disgusted by what she interpreted as a further demonstration of Charles' stupid incompetence. In fact, however, the fault was not entirely Bovary's although no one recognized this. Some of the blame also belonged to the specialist who had published an untested and undependable "cure."

Bovary and Emma were both depressed by this incident, although for different reasons. He was ashamed of what he had done and felt that he had been irresponsible. She reproached herself for ever having had faith in him and decided that she was now absolved of any responsibility to her husband. Her passion for Rodolphe flared up again, and she saw him that night for the first time in many days. Charles, in his simplicity, assumed that Emma's depression had been caused by sympathy for him and was gratified by her demonstration of devotion.

Comment

A.

This chapter interrupts the progress of the love affair. At the end of the last chapter, Emma had begun to repent of her love for Rodolphe. Now she turns to Charles, and when Homais suggests the operation, she encourages it thinking that if Charles were famous she could respect him. Through it all, Homais and Emma never give any thought to Charles or to Hippolyte, but instead see in the operation how they could personally benefit from the fame. *We* know, and later in retrospect Emma realizes, that Charles is not capable of such an operation, and it is only through the goading of Emma and Homais that he ever consents. The operation having failed, Emma now repents of her past virtue. In other words, Charles' ineptitude and stupidity now give her full justification to carry out her affair with no tinge of recrimination. Thus this interlude functions to again convince Emma of Charles' ignorance and to justify her infidelity.

B.

The description of the operation, the gangrene with its smell, the interest of the crowd, and the suffering of Hippolyte are all masterfully rendered. And the absurdity of Homais' letter composed immediately after the operation should be compared with the equally absurd letter describing the agricultural show in chapter 8.

PART II – CHAPTERS 12 & 13

Summary

The liaison between Emma and Rodolphe began again and now evolved with greater ardor. As her passion for Rodolphe increased, Emma found that she disliked Bovary even more, and she began to speak vaguely of leaving him someday. When she was not with Rodolphe, Emma suffered from boredom and was irritated by all of Charles' mannerisms and acts. She began to feel sorry for herself because of her unhappy marriage and found some solace in catering to her material desires. She fell an easy victim to the wily merchant, Lheureux, who cajoled her into many purchases that she could not afford.

Rodolphe, meanwhile, was growing tired of Emma. The novelty of her love was wearing off, and her ridiculous whims annoyed him.

Bovary's mother paid the family a visit. She and Emma had their usual fight, though Emma was finally induced by Charles to apologize. She was mortified by this and when she saw Rodolphe that night, Emma asked him to take her away from all her misery. He reminded her of the baby, and as an afterthought, Emma decided to take the child with her.

In the next few days Bovary and his mother were amazed and pleased at the changes that came over Emma; she was quiet and docile now and seemed a new person. But at her secret meetings with Rodolphe, Emma was planning to run away and start her life again. The happiness that such plans gave her added new highlights and softness to her beauty. She was so gentle and lovely that Bovary was reminded of the first days of their marriage, and his love for her and Berthe deepened. Emma's thoughts, though, were always far off, contemplating exotic lands and adventures.

Despite Rodolphe's procrastination, the final plans for their departure were made. He and Emma would leave Yonville separately, meet in Rouen, and then go on together to Paris. On the night before the day selected, they met in Emma's garden to make the last arrangements. Emma was in high spirits and seemed more beautiful than ever. Rodolphe was reserved and thoughtful. After leaving her he argued with himself for a while. The problems and burdens of life with Emma, he decided, would not be worth the sensual pleasure she could offer him.

That night Rodolphe sat at his desk and mused for a while about the many women he had known. After some trouble he composed a letter which he felt would end their affair with the fewest complications. He wrote her that he loved her very much (which was not true) and that this was why he was abandoning her. He said that the life he could offer would provide her only with pain and indignity, and he could not bear to do this. And, he thought, this was really not too far from the truth after all. Much satisfied with his work, Rodolphe went to sleep.

Emma received this note the next morning and became faint from shock. In her confusion she dropped the crumbled up letter in the attic and forgot about it. Rodolphe had told her that he was leaving Yonville to protect her from him, and a few moments later she saw his carriage drive by. This awful reminder of what had just happened was like a blow to her heart. She screamed aloud and fell unconscious.

Emma became seriously ill. She had a high fever and delirium for 43 days and was often close to death. Bovary never left her side and neglected all his affairs to care for her. Specialists were called in from Rouen and elsewhere, and every effort was made to cure her, but for a long time nothing had any success.

By October Emma began to regain her strength. She still had fainting spells and weak periods, but she was able to move around a little, and was clearly on the road to recovery.

Comment

A.

These two chapters present the passionate renewal of Emma and Rodolphe's love affair after the disappointing interlude connected with Hippolyte's foot. Emma's romanticism now forces her to bring the romance to a climax. She is not satisfied with having an affair with Rodolphe. She insists that they flee together to some strange land. This emphasis on flight is another romantic concept. And while she is insisting that they go away, she begins to go deeper in debt to Lheureux by ordering expensive gifts for Rodolphe and the necessary things for the trip.

B.

After Emma receives Rodolphe's letter, she immediately begins to think of suicide. This foreshadows her actual suicide later on.

C.

Emma's sickness caused by her betrayal suggests that perhaps she felt a love for Rodolphe that is indeed deeper than that of a common woman. Perhaps Flaubert is here indicating that Emma, in spite of her romanticism, is capable of a deep devotion. But most critics prefer to read this scene as Emma's reaction to the loss of her dream and the realization of the emptiness and uselessness of life without her dream. Her sickness, therefore, is simply a result of the betrayal and the loss of her ideal which brings to her the realization that she must continue the empty life that she had lived before her encounter with Rodolphe.

D.

It should be noted here that in spite of Charles' dullness and stupidity, he does possess a dogged devotion to Emma. He gives up his practice and remains by her side during her entire illness. Of course, it could be said that his devotion is the same that an animal would have for his master, but it is, nevertheless, a redeeming characteristic in Charles' otherwise flat personality.

PART II – CHAPTERS 14 & 15

Summary

In addition to his concern about Emma, Charles was also bothered by financial worries. The illness had been very expensive, and other bills were piling up. Moreover, Lheureux suddenly presented him with a statement of Emma's debts. Not knowing what else to do, Bovary borrowed money from Lheureux and signed several notes at a high rate of interest.

All through the winter months Emma's convalescence continued. During a crisis in her illness, Emma's religious sentiments had reawakened. Now she was very devout and spent much of her time reading religious books or conversing with the priest.

By spring Emma was relatively strong again and returned to her household duties. Her religious feelings remained firm, and everyone was surprised by her new generosity, spirituality, and stern principles.

One day at Homais' suggestion, Bovary decided to take Emma to the theater at Rouen. He hoped that such an outing would be good for her health. Emma was not eager to go, but Bovary was so persistent that she agreed. On the day of the trip they excitedly left for the city.

Emma was embarrassed and upset by Charles' behavior and appearance all that afternoon. She wanted very much to seem a sophisticated, cosmopolitan lady, and she felt that he was just a country bumpkin. She was tense and self-conscious wherever they went. Despite this, however, Emma enjoyed the opera, *Lucie de Lammermoor*, very much. She found that the story reminded her of events in her own life.

During the intermission they were both surprised to encounter Leon, who now lived and worked in Rouen. The three went to a cafe together, where Bovary and Leon talked at length about Yonville, their mutual friends, and old times. Leon also told them a little about his present position and his experiences at the university. Emma was impressed by Leon's suave, citified manners and dress. When they discussed the opera they had just left, Leon at first ridiculed it until he learned that perhaps Emma could stay over to see the second part again. He then praised the opera so highly that Charles suggested that Emma stay while he return to his practice. In any case, before they separated, the Bovarys and Leon arranged to meet again the next day.

Comment

A.

After Emma's recovery from her illness, she falls back into the old established neurotic pattern of taking up something (this time religion) only to drop it for something else. She gave herself so completely to religion that even the curé thought she went too far. Then she began charity work even though her own household needed attention.

B.

Once at the opera, Emma becomes immersed in the romantic world on the stage. She begins to identify with the heroine and she is entranced with the tenor. Here Flaubert's art is very subtle. The objective description of the artist says little, but implies that the artist is false. Like Emma, he misrepresents art. He uses tricks to cover up for his lack of art. There is "something of the hair dresser and the toreador" about him. Thus, Emma is lost in this false and sentimental world of cheap art.

C.

The scene at the opera prepares the reader and also Emma for the reintroduction of Leon. The romantic elements of the opera provide an apt meeting place to rekindle their attraction to each other.

PART III – CHAPTER 1

Summary

While attending law school in Paris, Leon was a model student. But he did experience a new way of life even though he remained quiet and respectable. And now that he has returned to Rouen, he has brought with him many of the manners and sophistication that he learned in Paris. He dressed and acted in the Parisian style and felt especially self-confident in Rouen, where he considered himself to be a sophisticate among the local provincials.

At first in Paris he had often thought about Emma, but gradually she became a blurred memory. Now his old feelings for her were reawakened. He visited Emma at her hotel the next day while Bovary was out.

She and Leon were pleased by this opportunity to see each other in private, and they held an animated conversation for several hours. Their old intimacy was renewed, although both withheld several personal details of their recent experiences. Emma and Leon recalled their sad parting in Yonville and the times they had spent together there and discussed with a new frankness their mutual affection. Before leaving, Leon kissed Emma, and they arranged to have a secret meeting at the cathedral the next day.

In the morning, Leon arrived punctually at the place of the rendezvous. Emma was late and tried at first to avoid him, for she hoped to prevent herself from falling in love with him again. She tried to pray but her mind was not on it. Then she readily accepted an invitation from the beadle of the church to see the various parts of the cathedral. Leon suffered the sightseeing as long as possible and then pulled Emma away from the church and into a carriage he had sent for.

The carriage driver could not understand why two people would want to ride aimlessly about the countryside on such a pretty day with all the curtains pulled. Every time he made an attempt to stop, he was severely reprimanded by Leon. They were together in the carriage so long that Emma missed the Hirondelle that was to take her back to Yonville. She had to hire a special hack to catch the Hirondelle before it reached Yonville.

Comment

A.

Chapter 1 presents Leon's background so as to show how he

has changed during the interim. He is no longer so retiring and bashful. Paris has given him a sense of self-assurance which will allow him now to approach Madame Bovary. But we should also note that even though both he and Emma have changed, their talk is still filled with commonplace romantic cliches and platitudes.

B.

Flaubert's description of the church where Leon is to meet Emma is a masterpiece of realistic description and subtle suggestion. Flaubert describes the church (particularly the chancery) in terms of a lady's boudoir where the church (or Emma) is waiting to "gather the confession of her love." These descriptions sum up everything about Emma's own religion — a religion which Emma sees only in her own way. Thus, after Emma enters, she immediately attempts to pray, but her thoughts are not on religion but instead on herself and her relationship with Leon. Throughout the entire scene, it is ironic that both Emma and Leon are seething with a burning passion while the slow bungling guide shows them through the cold ancient church. Their view of the huge, magnificent church should be contrasted with the final scene, that of Emma and Leon riding in a small closed carriage while consummating their love. The carriage is even described as being "sealed tighter than a tomb," and if the image is extended, this is the beginning of Emma's last fated episode which will lead to her suicide.

PART III — CHAPTERS 2, 3, & 4

Summary

On her return to Yonville, Emma learned that Bovary's father had died. Charles was very upset, particularly because he had not seen the man in a long time. Emma felt no sorrow but made the usual sympathetic gestures, which her husband misunderstood and appreciated very much. After a while, Mrs. Bovary came to stay with them. Emma was polite and attentive but was annoyed because the necessity for being kind to the mourners distracted her from thoughts of Leon.

At about this time Lheureux made another appearance and presented Emma with her unpaid bills. He also managed to sell her some more high priced merchandise. When Emma expressed a worry about managing to pay, he suggested that she get a Power of Attorney from Bovary. That way, he said, she would not have to bother her husband with "petty" financial matters and could find a convenient method to settle her debts.

Emma convinced Bovary of the wisdom of this scheme without too much trouble, since he had no idea of the true amount of their debts. Emma even induced him to use the services of Leon, instead of the local attorney, for drawing up the papers, and Bovary trustingly arranged to send her alone to Rouen to take care of this business.

Emma spent the next three days in Rouen with Leon. He rented an expensive hotel room for the occasion, and this short period was like a honeymoon for them. They went to some of the best restaurants and places of entertainment and spent most of their time in lovemaking and romantic pursuits.

Leon became completely involved in his affair with Emma; he neglected his work and saw little of his friends. The arrival of her letters became a major event in his life, and he even paid a few visits to Yonville, either in secret or on various false pretexts, to see her.

Emma, meanwhile, was getting even more deeply enmeshed in financial obligations to Lheureux. In order to see Leon more often, she began to show a renewed interest in the piano, and soon got Bovary to arrange for her to take a weekly lesson with a teacher in Rouen.

Comment

A.

Before Emma can continue with her affair with Leon, she is interrupted by the death of her father-in-law. Then she must think of some plan whereby she can get back to Rouen and Leon. Monsieur Lheureux gives her the pretext. Knowing how easily he can convince Emma to buy things from him, he tells her to get Charles' power of attorney. His plan is to eventually foreclose on everything and thereby make a large profit. But his suggestions offer to Emma a pretext for going to Rouen to consult with Leon. So she convinces Charles that she should handle everything.

B.

The very short Chapter 3 covers the three days Emma spent with Leon in Rouen. The three days were described as "a real honeymoon." But the readers should remember that this is the *third* one. The episode is described in romantic terms of bliss and joy. For these few days, the image of beauty and innocence was restored to Emma, but the scene ends on an uglier note. Amid her renewed joys, she is reminded of her sordid affair with Rodolphe by hearing the boatman relate how Rodolphe had taken the same ride last week with some other lady.

C.

The short fourth chapter shows Emma and Leon continuing in their plans to make their meetings definite, and to meet at least once a week. This of course means that Emma will have to go deeper in debt.

PART III – CHAPTERS 5 & 6

Summary
    On the days of her lessons, Emma occupied all her time with Leon. Each week they had a passionate reunion, as if they had been separated for an age instead of for a few days. These visits were joyous events for both of them and were marked by profound emotional and romantic feelings. As their affair progressed, they viewed each other as if they were the idealized figures of sentimental fiction and attempted to enact all that once they had only imagined.

    Emma's departure was always a sorrowful moment, and the happiness she gained from seeing Leon disappeared as soon as the coach left Rouen. At home Emma was irritable and tense. She lived only for her next meeting with Leon and spent the week reading romantic books and reliving her memories, in order to keep her ardor at a high pitch.

Once she was nearly caught in her lie when Bovary ran into her supposed piano teacher and the woman did not recognize Emma's name. However, she was able to show Charles falsified receipts for the lessons and soon convinced him that nothing was wrong. Another time Lheureux saw her and Leon together in Rouen. She was afraid that he would tell Bovary, but instead the crafty merchant used her fright to force her into signing additional notes and selling some of Bovary's father's estate at a loss. Meanwhile, Emma was regularly being presented with other unpaid and overdue bills. She was confused by all this and unable to settle matters; so she attempted to ignore her creditors. She borrowed more and more from Lheureux, for as she became more worried and frightened, she also became more extravagant. She seemed to have no conception of the obligations incurred from borrowing money and hoped to forget her troubles through the possession of all sorts of wasteful luxuries. As a result, she went heavily into debt.

Despite her torrid affair with Leon, Emma was rapidly becoming unhappy again. Nothing meant anything to her any more except her Thursday in Rouen. She indulged in complicated sentimental excesses and wild flights of fantasy. In the desperate hope of finding happiness, she became voluptuous and greedy and tried to experience every kind of sensual pleasure. Nothing satisfied her, and her frustration increased. Her behavior perplexed Leon, particularly when she tried to force him to dress or act in certain ways or to quit his job in order to ensure his permanent devotion to her.

In the earliest stages of this affair, Emma had found contentment, and her mellow mood was reflected at home where she had been a considerate and dutiful wife. Now she was impossible to get along with again. Once she stayed overnight in Rouen with Leon and did not bother to inform Charles of her whereabouts. He was very worried and set out to find her. Later on she managed to convince the poor man that he was at fault for worrying and inquiring about her, and that there was nothing wrong with her strange behavior.

During Leon's visits to Yonville he had dined at the house of Homais, his old landlord. In return for this hospitality he felt obligated to invite Homais to Rouen. Homais eventually accepted the invitation and decided by coincidence, to come on the same day that Emma usually went to the city.

Once in Rouen, Homais sought out Leon and insisted that the young man accompany him to a restaurant and other places. Leon was not too assertive, and Homais easily quieted all his objections. Meanwhile, Emma waited impatiently in the hotel room. Leon managed to slip away from Homais for a little while to see her, but there was a nasty scene. She refused to listen to his excuses and accused him of such ridiculous things as preferring Homais to her. She returned to Yonville in a state of anger and began mentally to seek out all Leon's weaknesses.

After a while Emma realized that Leon was not really to blame for his conduct, but her awareness of his faults remained. She began to see that he was not the ideal figure she had imagined, and this thought troubled her. Their relationship was already shaky, and now it began to depend almost entirely on sensuality and various outside diversions that had once been secondary to their emotional feelings. In a frantic effort to regain the security of happiness, Emma sought to dominate all aspects of Leon's life. He resented her demands, and their moments of contentment were briefer than ever.

One day a debt collector called on Emma to get payment on one of her notes to Lheureux. Emma did not fully understand the meaning of his visit and made some feeble promises. The next afternoon she was served with a legal notice from the sheriff of the district. Emma was terrified and went to Lheureux. He was curt with her. After a while he relented, and though he claimed he could not afford the risk, he finally lent her more money on stiff terms and again tricked her into buying some expensive merchandise.

Emma was aroused by this experience and began an economy campaign. She cut down on household expenses, urged Bovary to get money from his mother, purchased little items in Rouen for re-sale to the ladies of Yonville, and secretly collected the money that was owned Bovary by his patients. She told her husband nothing about the real state of their finances. Despite all her efforts, Emma was unable to stop borrowing and continued to run up debts.

With this new burden added to her other troubles, Emma became temperamental and slovenly. The Bovary house was a melancholy place because she sold so many things to raise money; the mending and washing were undone, and the needs of the child were usually ignored. Emma had few friends any more and spent most of her time locked in her room. Bovary was worried and tried to comfort her, but she refused to speak with him and was unresponsive to all his clumsy advances.

Emma continued seeing Leon in Rouen and insisted on spending those days extravagantly. Leon often could not afford to entertain her in the style which she demanded; so she provided him with money, even when it meant pawning some of her possessions. Leon's family and friends had been urging him to end the affair, since they were concerned about its adverse effect upon his career and reputation. Now that Emma was becoming so moody and difficult, he started to agree with them and began to view her as a burden. Their relationship went on, but both of them often felt a secret disgust for each other, and even their lovemaking was now usually a source of boredom. In addition, Emma degraded herself by frequenting disreputable places and keeping low company, although she was ashamed afterwards. Her tastes and fancies became decadent and corrupt.

At last Emma was served with a court order, enjoining her to pay the sum of 8,000 francs or suffer confiscation of her household property. She ran to Lheureux and made wild promises, but he callously refused to help her any longer and sent her away.

Comment

A.

These two chapters present Emma's entry into another love affair and her forthcoming destruction. These two chapters evoke many comparisons and contrasts. In the beginning of the affair, she again saw herself as the "woman in love of all the novels, the heroine of all the dramas, the shadowy 'she' of all the poetry-books." This was the same as in the beginning of her romance with Rodolphe. But along with this similarity, we see Emma going to meet her lover by "going through alleyways and emerging" in disreputable parts of towns. Strong hints of ugliness pervade these meetings.

But as the affair progresses, we suddenly realize that the role Emma played with Rodolphe is suddenly reversed. Now Leon is in the place of Emma and Emma is playing the role that Rodolphe earlier acted. Now Emma is the experienced partner introducing the young and inexperienced Leon into love making and as Rodolphe used to come to her, now she goes to Leon. At the end of the day, it is Emma who must dress and make the journey home. Finally, even Leon realizes that he has "become her mistress rather than she his."

B.
During the first part of their relationship, Emma thought that she had found what she had been searching for during her whole life. But as the relationship progressed, she gradually began to realize that she couldn't look at Leon realistically. "Idols must not be touched; the gilt comes off on our hands." And she also realizes that she had made him seem to be more than he is. Then she wonders what causes "this inadequacy in her life." At home she would try to read romantic fiction hoping that the idealized heroes would re-awaken a love for Leon. But she had to finally admit that she was tired of him. She "had rediscovered in adultery all the banality of marriage." This discovery then seems to leave Emma more empty than ever.

C.
During her affair with Leon, she has continued to neglect her business and is steadily becoming more entangled in financial affairs. Flaubert seems to be correlating Emma's deteriorating moral sense with her financial deterioration. She becomes the pathological liar both about her affair with Leon and about the financial debts. And as the love affair begins to fail, her debts begin to confront her as though they were analogous to her entangled love life.

D.
Even in the early parts of Emma's affair with Leon, an ominous note appears. It is in the form of the old beggar, whom Emma often

meets immediately after leaving Leon. The ugliness and vulgar appearance, the degradation of this old blind beggar contrast well with the artificial bliss with which Emma has enfolded herself, and also serve to foreshadow the depths of degradation to which Emma is falling. He can even be said to be symbolic of the ugly death that Emma is soon to face. Emma then sinks to her lowest shortly after this when she goes to a masquerade party and ends up with low class clerks in an inferior eating house.

PART III – CHAPTER 7

Summary
In the morning the sheriff's officers arrived and made a complete inventory of the household furnishings and goods, but Emma managed to maintain a stoic attitude all the time they were there. They left a guard on the premises, but she kept him hidden in the attic where Bovary would not see him. That evening Bovary seemed worried, and Emma fearfully imagined that he knew, but he said nothing. She was particularly resentful that she bore all the responsibility in this matter and that Bovary was innocent. As the night passed, she occupied herself in making plans to raise the money.

The next morning Emma went to Rouen and called on several bankers, but they all refused to make a loan to her. She asked Leon for help, but he protested that he could never raise such a large sum and became angry when she suggested that he steal the money from his employer. Finally, in order to quiet her, Leon promised that he would see his friends, and if he could raise the sum she required, he would bring it to Yonville.

On Monday, Emma was horrified to discover that a public notice of the sheriff's confiscation and auction had been posted in the market place. She went to see Guillaumin, the town lawyer. He offered to help her, but made it clear that he expected favors from her in return. Emma was insulted by his forwardness, shouted that she was not for sale, and left in a fury.

Bovary was not home and still did not know what had taken place. Meanwhile, the entire town watched expectantly to see what would happen next. Emma felt weak and afraid; she kept hoping that Leon would gallop up with the money but really had no confidence in this possibility. She was bitter and frightened. Suddenly an idea came to her — Rodolphe — and she set out for his estate. She planned to take advantage of his supposed love for her and get the money from him. It never occurred to her that what she was planning to do was actually prostitution; exactly what she had so angrily refused when Guillaumin had made the same suggestion.

Comment

This chapter presents Emma's frantic efforts to obtain money from almost any source. She first goes to her latest lover, Leon; but since Leon is rather anxious to break with Emma, he proves to be of little help. In fact, he hurriedly gets rid of Emma by promising to do something the next day. Her failure is again represented by the appearance of the blind man. This time Homais gives the man a lecture and Emma throws him a half crown piece, the "sum of her wealth." Now she is totally destitute.

At the suggestion of her maid, Emma goes to see the lawyer, Monsieur Guillaumin, who supposedly was infatuated with Emma. He offers to give her the money, but she is expected to sleep with him. Emma is horrified and leaves in disgust. There is here a nobility in Emma's make-up. For all of her love affairs, she has never prostituted herself and totally rejects the idea. All of her love affairs have been an attempt to fulfill her dreams.

PART III — CHAPTER 8

Summary

Rodolphe was surprised to see Emma. They talked about the past for a while, and she was able, as planned, to arouse his old interest in her. She told him about her debts and asked him to lend her several thousand francs. Rodolphe began to understand the reason for her strange visit and calmly told her that he had no money available. Emma knew he was lying. She lost her temper and left.

Now Emma realized that the situation was hopeless. She walked through the fields without seeing and had dazed memories of incidents in her life. Then she became lucid again and decided what she had to do. She ran to Homais' shop and induced the servant, Justin, to let her into the attic. There she opened a jar of arsenic and ate a large quantity of it, while the frightened boy watched. She went home again, for the first time in a long while feeling at peace.

Meanwhile, Bovary had learned about the sheriff's confiscation. He searched frantically for Emma, but no one knew her whereabouts. When he returned home, he found her resting in bed. She gave him a letter which he was not to read until the next day.

In a short time Emma was torn by spasms of nausea and became violently ill. Despite his concern, she would tell Bovary nothing; so he opened her letter and discovered to his horror that she had poisoned herself. He called for help and soon the news spread through the town.

Homais came to his assistance, and they sent for doctors from Rouen and a neighboring town. Bovary was too upset to do anything and sat at Emma's bedside crying. She wept also and for once was tender to him. The other doctors and the priest arrived, but nothing could be done. After a few more hours, Emma died in great pain.

Comment

A.

When Emma arrives at Rodolphe's house to ask for money, the reader should remember that they haven't seen each other for over three years. Thus when he first sees Emma, all of his old desires for her are re-awakened and Emma is aware that she has some effect on him. Thus in his refusal to give her money, Emma feels that this is again a betrayal of her love. Flaubert intimates that Emma's desire to kill herself comes, not from her desperate financial condition and not from the weak Leon's refusal, but from a larger sense of betrayal by Rodolphe. To Emma, who has devoted her life to a search for perfect love, this second betrayal by Rodolphe makes life not worth living. Her reactions and her state of mind immediately after leaving Rodolphe are practically the same as when he first betrayed her. And as she was sick for forty-three days on the first time, she decides now to take her life. Thus Emma's suicide is motivated by her sense of betrayal by the one man whom she might have loved. Flaubert perhaps is suggesting that Emma was capable of a profound love. If she was not, then at least, she possessed a dream of love which was worth living for and when this dream was betrayed, there was nothing left but suicide.

B.

It is a bit of Flaubert's irony that Justin is directly responsible for Emma's death. This is ironic because he is the one character in the book who has demonstrated a constant, undeviating love for Emma. His love for Emma exists on a plane which Emma herself never felt and never achieved; thus it is ironic that the person who most loved and adored her was also the one responsible for her death. That is, had he not loved her so much, he would never have been intimidated enough so as to give her the keys to the secret room where the arsenic was kept.

C.

Emma's death reflects the pathetic misuse of her life. As she has spent her life longing for the unattainable and had failed miserably, so in death she longed for a simple but beautiful death. But instead, her death is one of horrible suffering and ugliness, and the ugliness of her death is emphasized by the appearance of the blind man, the symbol of her degradation in life.

D.

Emma's last act is that of taking extreme unction, and this act captures the essence of the novel. Here she returns to the religious fold, but her return is in terms of sensuousness. The kiss that she gives to the crucifix is not one given to God but it is more of an erotic, sensual kiss. And when the priest anoints her, Flaubert subtly reminds the reader that this woman is a sensualist: the priest anoints the eyes "that had coveted all worldly pomp" then the nostrils and mouth "that had uttered lies, that had curled with pride and cried out in lewdness;" then the hands that "had delighted in sensual touches," and finally the feet which were "so swift...when she was running to satisy her desires, and that would now walk no more." Thus the final picture of Emma is that of the sensualist looking in death for the supreme sensual desire.

E.

Many critics have suggested that with the appearance of Dr. Lariviere we have our only admirable character in the novel. Perhaps this characterization is influenced by Flaubert's own father. He does contrast to the other characters, in view of the fact that he is coldly analytical, but yet his presence indicates that he cares for humanity. He does express real sympathy for his patients; and his sense of intelligence, his professional dignity, and his integrity set off all the other characters as being petty and stupid.

PART III – CHAPTERS 9, 10 & 11

Summary
It took Charles a long time to recover from the initial shock of Emma's death. His mother arrived and helped to put affairs in order, and thought that now Emma was gone she would be reinstated in Charles' affection. Emma's father also showed up for the funeral, but was too emotional to be of help. The priest and Homais sat up all night with the body and performed certain rites which they thought appropriate. The priest had a difficult time convincing Charles that the burial should take place soon. Charles gave directions for Emma to be buried in her wedding dress and quarrelled with his mother about the expense of some parts of the funeral.

As soon as the funeral is over, old Rouault goes home without even seeing little Berthe. Later that night the sexton sees Justin by Emma's grave and thinks that he now knows who has been stealing his potatoes.

In the days which followed, Bovary was contacted by all Emma's creditors. Her debts included not merely those of Lheureux, but many bills to business concerns, tradesmen, and other people.

Their total constituted a vast amount. Bovary tried to collect the fees due him in an effort to pay but learned that Emma had already done so.

In the meantime, Leon became engaged to a young woman of good family. Bovary sent a letter of congratulations to Leon's mother, in which he remarked, innocently, that the news would have pleased his late wife.

One night Bovary came across the letter from Rodolphe that Emma had lost in the attic a long time before. He read it, but assumed that there had been a platonic affection between them and was not concerned. He idealized Emma's memory and was pleased to learn that another had also admired her.

In an attempt to pay his debts, Bovary had to sell nearly all the furniture, but even this amount was not sufficient. For sentimental reasons, though, he refrained from taking anything from her bedroom and kept it just the way it was before her death. Mrs. Bovary had come to live with him, but they had a quarrel over the possession of one of Emma's shawls and she left his house. The servant left also, taking most of Emma's wardrobe with her.

Bovary began to live in seclusion. He avoided his old friends and neglected his practice. Homais, who had once been so close, and who was now a power in the community, shunned him, claiming that there was too big a gap in their social positions.

Bovary often sat in Emma's room, examining her possessions and recalling their life together. One day he opened her desk and discovered the letters from Rodolphe and Leon. He read them with an air of disbelief and was very distressed when he realized their meaning and was forced to acknowledge that Emma had been unfaithful. After this he was always gloomy and seemed a broken man. He rarely left his house and kept away from people.

Once he had to go to Rouen to sell his horse in order to raise more money. He met Rodolphe there and the two men had a drink together in a cafe. Rodolphe felt guilty and tried to make small talk. Finally Bovary told him that he knew the truth, but that he no longer held any grudge against him. The fault, Bovary said, was with Destiny.

The next day Bovary died quietly while sitting in his garden. His house and remaining property were sold on behalf of his creditors, and there was just enough left over to send Berthe to stay with her grandmother. Mrs. Bovary died later that year and Roualt was seriously ill; so Berthe was then sent to an aunt's house. This woman was very poor, and the little girl ended up working in a cotton mill.

Comment

A.

The final chapters are concerned with showing the effect of Emma's death on various people. The greatest effect is on Charles who mourns her death for a long time before he discovers the letters from Rodolphe and Leon. Then he slowly deteriorates in despair and poverty and inertia. Obliquely, Emma's death probably has the greatest effect on little Berthe, since at the age of seven she is sent into the cotton mill to earn her own living. In contrast, the people whom she most loved, Rodolphe and Leon, are not at all affected by her death. Justine who loved her with the purest love, is accused of stealing potatoes because he returned to cry at her grave.

B.

The last chapter is filled with many ironies. That Charles would want to bury Emma in her wedding dress (symbol of purity) is ironic in view of Emma's infidelities. The actions of the chemist and the priest are developed to show how their every act is not for someone else's benefit but for their own advancement. Homais' receipt of the cross of the Legion of Honor suggests the pettiness of the society against which Emma revolted.

C.

So in the final analysis, as seen against the society in which Emma lived, Emma becomes a rather sympathetic character. She was a woman who had a full conviction of her dreams and was willing to risk everything for them. She had a glimpse of a life and of emotions that exist outside this narrow provincial world, but her tragedy lies finally in the fact that she could find no object in this world worthy of her dreams.

CHARACTER ANALYSIS

Emma Bovary

(For additional help in analyzing Emma, see especially the comments after the following chapters: Part I, Chapters 6 and 9; Part II, Chapters 9 and 10.)

Emma's early life influenced her entire approach to life. She was born with a natural tendency toward sentimentality. She preferred the dream world to the real world. Rather than being brought up in the realities of everyday living, she was sent when very young to a convent where she indulged in daydreams and in sentimentalizing about life. Here at the convent, she began reading romance novels which affected her entire life. In religion, she searched for the unusual, the mystic, and the beautiful rather than for the real essence of the church. Being basically a dreamy girl, she developed into the extreme romantic who spent her time longing and sighing for old castles, secret meetings, and intrigues. She closed her eyes to the real world and attempted to force life to conform with her romantic fiction. She constantly felt the need for excitement and could not endure the dull routine of everyday living.

After her marriage, Emma continued in her search for excitement. She could not tolerate her marriage because it did not fit into the fictionalized accounts that she had read about. She missed the bliss, ecstasy, and passion that she hoped she would find in marriage. And rather than devoting herself to living life, rather than facing reality, she hid herself in her dreams and expended all of her energy in futile longings. She was continually dissatisfied with her life and searched constantly for ways to change things.

Thus, since life refused to conform to her romantic picture, Emma began to alternate between various things in the hope that her unfulfilled longings would be satisfied. She tried everything. She redecorated the house, she took up reading, subscribed to Parisian magazines, helped at charities, knitted, painted, played the piano, and engaged in a multitude of other activities. But with each thing she attempted, she soon became bored and rejected one activity for another. This frenzied search for excitement exhausted her until she made herself physically sick.

Charles' own sense of complacency and his dullness only added to Emma's misfortune. Thus when she met Leon, she felt that she had found her soul mate. She was unable to see that her thoughts and his were both part of the same romantic concept expressed in platitudes and cliches. She mistook superficiality in Leon for profundity. They became platonic friends. After he left, Emma felt that she had missed something, that something had been denied her. Therefore, later when she meets Rodolphe, she is ready to give herself to him readily. She had longed for someone who would "know about everything, excel in a multitude of activity," and who would introduce her "to passions in all its force, to life in all its graces," and initiate her "into all mysteries." Thus, when Rodolphe appears and begins his frank, daring and passionate exclamations of love, Emma feels that she is now experiencing these passions and these elemental forces. He is then the fulfillment of her dreams. For the first time, she feels that her life now has all the "passion, ecstasy and delirium" of the romances which she had read.

Emma's nature will not allow her to remain in one situation. She begins to want to change things. As she changed from knitting to painting, etc., so now she wants to change things with Rodolphe. She insists that they run off together. This insistence causes Rodolphe to drop her.

After her recovery from Rodolphe's betrayal, Emma meets Leon again and gives herself to him rather readily. She is still searching for that noble passion. But true to Emma's nature, she soon begins to tire of Leon and becomes once again bored with life. She found in "adultery all the banality of marriage."

Thus Emma Bovary was a middle class woman who could not stand the middle-class life. She spent her entire life in an attempt to escape from this middle-class existence by dreams, love affairs, and false pretentions.

Emma possesses one quality that the other characters do not have. She has a dream of life that allows her to look for ideals and feelings greater than she is. Even though these ideals might be superficial, she is aware that there are feelings greater than those found in her middle-class surroundings. And in spite of her infidelities, she could not give herself in prostitution in order to solve her financial situation. She remained true to her dreams and she died by her dreams. After her second interview with Rodolphe, she felt that she had been betrayed anew and felt that only in death could she find the peace and fulfillment that she had been searching for. Thus, she tried to live by her dreams, and when that failed, she died by them without ever compromising her vision of something greater than she.

Charles Bovary

Charles is the dull, unimaginative country doctor. From the opening chapters, we are made aware that Charles must work very diligently at something that comes easily for others. He lacks the dashing imagination that characterizes his father, the elder Bovary. His constant struggle to achieve almost anything is a part of his essential nature. He has no natural talents and must work twice as hard as others in order to achieve the simplest results.

In his school, we saw that when he relaxes he gives himself over to aimless wanderings and ultimately fails his examinations. Furthermore, he is the type who can be easily controlled by a woman. First, his mother ruled his life completely for him, even arranging a marriage for him with a woman about twenty years older than he. Thus his first wife was able to rule him rather easily. But these women make it exceptionally easy for Emma to control Charles and to get her way in every matter.

Charles functions as a complete contrast to Emma. His plodding nature and his routine ardors and embraces suggest his insensitive nature. He is content with the commonplace activities and is too dull to notice Emma's dissatisfaction. He assumes that

Emma is as happy as he is, and he is incapable of detecting any subtle differences in their life. Whereas Emma burns to experience everything in life, Charles feels that with the birth of his daughter, he has now gone through the complete list of human experiences. His contentment with his life only makes life more unbearable for Emma.

Charles' only attribute is his devoted love for Emma. His every concern is directed toward her happiness and his love and devotion are completely unselfish. When Emma is sick, he leaves all else and devotes himself entirely to her recovery. He is, then, capable of unselfish feelings whereas Emma is concerned only with herself.

Charles is, then, the dull commonplace little man, the typical representative of the insensitive and unimaginative human being. He was intended by Flaubert to personify many of the most appalling aspects of provincial, middle class society.

Leon
When Emma first meets Leon, she feels that she has found a kindred spirit. But we know that Leon is as superficial as is Emma. Both are distinguished from the other members of the society because both strive for some feelings that transcend this society. But both are also trapped in their own romantic dreams.

At first Leon is terribly shy and unsure of himself. He is inexperienced in the world of women and love. He has lived too long in a world of sentimental romantic fantasy. Thus when confronted with Emma, he cannot bring himself to tell her of his real feelings. His fears overcome him, and he is afraid of being ridiculous.

After Leon has been to Paris, he gains more confidence in himself. When he returns to Paris, he retains many of the Parisian manners and "airs," giving the impression that he is really the master of any situation. Thus when he meets Emma again after three years separation, he has acquired a thin veneer of sophistication, but he is still a shallow and weak young man. Even though he begins a love affair with Emma, he realizes himself that he is not the master of the situation. He is unable to act in an aggressive or decisive manner and allows Emma to lead in their relationship.

Furthermore, Leon also serves to illustrate the divergence between Emma's dreams and her reality. She forces Leon to conform to her idealized concept of a lover. She refuses for a long time to face reality, and the contrast between Flaubert's objective description of the weak, fluctuating Leon and Emma's idealized conception of him underlines Emma's predicament.

Rodolphe

Rodolphe is the only person in the novel who understands Emma. He is basically a shrewd and cynical bachelor who has spent his time studying the psychology of women with the sole purpose of seducing them. When he first met Emma, he knew immediately that she was bored with her husband and was ready for a love affair. He met her often enough to get her excited with his straight, direct declarations of love. He knew that she wanted to hear fanciful exaggerated things, and he accommodated her. Then he disappears for six weeks so as to let Emma worry and fret. When he reappears, it is no trouble to carry out the seduction.

But Rodolphe is not interested in any affair for very long. He is interested only in his own sensual enjoyment and his only worry is how to break off his love affairs after he tires of them. His attraction toward Emma is founded only on her good looks and her sensuous appeal. Thus, he has no qualms about seducing her and later abandoning her. He is even able to rationalize his motives so well that he feels no guilt about the episode. Upon learning of Emma's death, he has no feelings one way or another. He is, therefore, the unemotional, sensuous individual concerned only with his own pleasures.

Homais

The apothecary at Yonville. He is one of the most successful supporting characters in the novel, because there is a complete identity between his function as a character and his function as the representative of a type. He stands for the new middle-class spirit and "progressive" outlook that Flaubert detested so much. Homais' intellect is limited, and he is poorly educated, but he is pretentious and puffed up with self-esteem. His talk consists of cliches and half-truths, and he demonstrates all the limitations and prejudices of the new bourgeoisie. For example, he is an avowed agnostic and an exponent of Voltaire, yet he is fearful and superstitious in the face of death. Furthermore, he is cowardly and irresponsible, as is shown in the aftermath of the episode concerning the operation on Hippolyte, and though he professes equalitarian principles, he is himself status conscious. Some of the best comic scenes in the novel are the conversations between Homais and his rival, the priest. Flaubert's pessimism is illustrated by the ending of the novel, where Homais' advancement and personal triumph are described.

CRITICAL PROBLEMS

THEME AND INTENT

Madame Bovary is a study of human stupidity and the "romantic malady," the despair and unhappiness faced by those who are unwilling or unable to resolve the conflicts between their dreams and idealized aspirations and the real world; in modern terms, one might say it is a study of a neurosis. Furthermore, it examines middle-class conventions and the myth of progress, exposing weaknesses and hypocrisies, and it deals with the inability of the different characters to communicate with each other. In all of these aspects, this novel is as pertinent in the mid-twentieth century as when it was written. The costumes and settings may change, but people do not, and human problems remain the same. As a matter of fact, some critics have pointed out the close relationship between Emma Bovary and the heroine of Sinclair Lewis' *Main Street,* for provincial life is the same everywhere, and these two women, despite their differences, are afflicted by many similar problems and frustrations.

Flaubert's characters are all ordinary people and are very much like ourselves and our neighbors. Nothing about them is romanticized or exalted, so that it is possible for the reader to see himself in a new and harsher light, and he cannot avoid sympathetic identification with them. The people of *Madame Bovary* are limited intellectually and culturally; they are sometimes sincere and well-intentioned, sometimes petty and vulgar, sometimes pathetic and confused, and sometimes unaware of the most obvious things or unable to take the most obvious action. They are so true to life that there are readers who resent the novel because they resent the uncomplimentary view that they are forced to take of themselves.

FLAUBERT'S REALISM

Madame Bovary is considered one of the finest "realistic" novels, and this is because of its unadorned, unromantic portrayals of everyday life and people. However, it must be understood that in literary realism one gets a view of the real world as seen through the eyes of the author. Throughout the novel there is a very carefully planned selection of episodes and incidents, so that "realism," if interpreted to mean a kind of journalistic reportage, is misleading. Every detail in *Madame Bovary* is chosen for a purpose and is closely related to everything else that precedes and follows it, to an extent that may not be evident (or possible) in real life. There is profound artistry involved in what is selected and omitted and in what weight is given to specific incidents.

The final greatness of Flaubert's realism lies in the manner in which he is able to capture the dullness of these middle class people without making his novel dull. Flaubert's minute attention to detail, his depiction of the average life, and his handling of the commonplace, all require the touch of the great artist, or else, this type of writing will degenerate into rather common dull prose. Flaubert was intent that every aspect of his novel would ring true to life. He visited the places which he wrote about to make certain that his descriptions were accurate. After he had written the Prefect's speech at the agriculture show, a speech very similar to Flaubert's was actually given by a district Prefect: both speeches were filled with the same platitudes and same cliches. And finally, Flaubert's handling of Homais is a masterful stroke of realistic description. He is able to select enough details to suggest to the reader how boring Homais' conversation is without having to repeat enough of what Homais actually said to bore the reader. And it is this selection of detail that marks Flaubert's genius.

SELECTION

An example of Flaubert's intentional selection of events takes place in III, Part I. Even that early in the novel, the reader is given a searching insight into the operation of Emma's mind and a portent of things to come, when the author comments:

> Emma, for her part, would have liked a marriage at midnight by the light of torches, but her father thought such an idea nonsensical.
>
> (trans. Gerard Hopkins)

This brief remark crystalizes the opposition between the sentimental romanticizing that will later cause Emma's downfall, and the unsympathetic real world, represented by her hard-headed peasant father.

A reporter must narrate his story as it occurs. He has no more insight or perspective than the participants, and he can only present random "slices of life," drawn out of context. Flaubert intended to illustrate a definite thesis by his story. Although his method was realistic, he determined where to place his emphasis and what to concentrate on by reference to this purpose.

SYMBOLISM

Flaubert also made extensive use of symbolism in his novel. Symbolic things are those which have an objective and limited function but which can be interpreted also to embody a wider and more profound meaning in regard to the things around them. In such a painstakingly constructed novel as *Madame Bovary,* it is rewarding to search for additional layers of meaning wherever the omission of a particular detail would not have affected the objective narration of the story. For instance, the complicated description of Charles' hat in the first chapter is not necessary to a realistic account of his school days, but has been shown to symbolize many aspects of his personality and future development. Other examples of symbols include the blind beggar, the wedding bouquet of Charles' first wife, and Emma's pet greyhound. Critics have pointed out that even the names of the characters in *Madame Bovary* have symbolic meanings; for example, Bovary is indeed bovine.

IRONY AND CONTRAST

Flaubert made use of irony and contrast on many planes, always with the intention of heightening his meaning and directing the reader's attention to his main themes. Each part of the novel contains pairs of contrasting scenes which clarify the reactions of the participants and the point of the story through their interaction. In Part I, these scenes are those describing the Bovarys' rustic wedding and the Marquis' grand ball. There are many other uses of irony, as in the contrast between the speeches of the Prefect's representative and Rodolphe at the Agricultural Show. The interrelationship of different episodes in the novel is shown at the end of Part II, where Emma develops an interest in the tenor Lagardy, emotionally preparing her and the reader for the unexpected entrance of Leon.

In terms of the entire novel, Charles had two wives who contrasted with each other. Emma had two lovers who are about as opposite as two people can be. But the greatest thematic contrast remains the contrast between Emma's idealized, fictionalized world and the realistic dull world in which she lives. This contrast embodies the differences between her hopes and her achievements. This is finally brought to an ugly conclusion when she desired a beautiful peaceful death, but instead suffered great agonies and endured great pain for hours before death finally came.

For additional analysis of this problem, consult PART II CHAPTER 8.

STYLE

Flauber was a very diligent and precise craftsman. He spent more than five years working on *Madame Bovary,* in the course of which he wrote biographies of all the characters and drew maps of the towns which were his settings. The original draft of the novel was several times longer than the completed version. Extensive research was applied to all features of the story, in order to guarantee a completely accurate picture of provincial life. While he was still writing the manuscript. Flaubert took great pride in learning that a phrase identical with one in the Prefect's speech actually appeared in a speech delivered by a government official in another part of the country.

Even the individual words Flaubert used were carefully selected, and he evoked additional subtleties of meaning and intensifications of mood from his skilled use of varied grammatical tenses and other rhetorical devices in the narrative. The pace of the novel is intricately related to the story, and the careful reader notes that events move with a speed related to the emotional feelings of the characters. When Emma is bored, her thoughts and activities are described in minute detail, and the reader becomes bored also. During Emma's frantic search for happiness in her liaison with Leon, she and the reader move through the events of several months in a bare few moments, emphasizing the transience of her pleasure.

NARRATIVE TECHNIQUE

Many of the techniques Flaubert used for descriptive purposes are cinematic in their quality, such as the flashing back and forth between the Prefect's speech and Rodolphe's flirting at the Agricultural Show. During the wild coach ride taken by Emma and Leon through the suburbs of Rouen, and at other points, the reader is made to view events from the outside. This adds to the air of reality, and it makes it necessary for the reader to call upon his own experiences to assist in understanding the experiences of the characters. The reader, in a sense, is made to participate with them. In addition, *Madame Bovary* has a formal structure that adds to the aesthetic quality of the story. Its three parts are comparable, in their development, exposition, and denouement, to the parts of a stage play, and the entire movement of the novel shows a theatrical sense of the dramatic.

SOCIAL COMMENTARY

In *Madame Bovary* Flaubert depicted an entire segment of society and unmercifully analyzed its people. He created unforgettable characters from whom our own age can learn valuable and essential lessons. Moreover, he took a mundane story and, thanks to his skill as a writer, demonstrated the potentialities of everyday life as a source of art. He was a leader in the trend towards realism in western literature. Before Flaubert, the novel was often rambling and discursive, but he helped to give it a definite structure and purpose and to make it acceptable in the canons of formal literature. There are faults in his work, for his characters are often not solid enough to bear the weight of their symbolic meanings, and Flaubert's extreme pessimism prevented him from being truly objective or fair in his evaluations and characterizations. Nonetheless, *Madame Bovary* is one of the greatest of novels and stands among the most treasured items in our living cultural heritage.

FLAUBERT'S LIFE AND WORKS

Gustave Flaubert was born December 12, 1821, in Rouen, France, and died May 8, 1880. He was the fourth child of a distinguished doctor who was the head of the hospital in that city. Gustave was a sensitive and quiet boy; he read a lot, and since the family lived in a house on the hospital grounds, he early gained a knowledge of scientific techniques and ideas. He attended a secondary school in Rouen, and in 1841 was sent, against his will, to study law in Paris. In the capital he made new friends and moved in literary circles. His talent for writing was stimulated by these experiences.

In 1844 Flaubert became the victim of a serious nervous illness, which cannot be identified precisely, but which was probably related to epilepsy. For reasons of health he retired to the family's new home in Le Croisset, a suburb of Rouen. He gladly took this opportunity to give up law and most of his time was now spent at Le Croisset where he lived quietly and devoted himself to writing and his studies.

Flaubert made a trip to the Near East in 1849-50, where he traveled widely in Egypt, Syria, Turkey, and Greece, and in 1857 he visited the site of ancient Carthage in North Africa. As the years passed, he became acquainted with most of the important literary figures of the period, including Victor Hugo, Georges Sand, Sainte-Beuve, Gautier, Turgenev, the de Goncourts, and de Maupassant. He was respected and admired by all of them.

Flaubert had few close friends, but there were two unusual relationships with women in his life. The first involved Elisa Schlessinger, a married older woman whom he met at Trouville when he was fifteen and who for many years was the object of his platonic and idealized affection. The other was Louise Colet, a poetess, who was his mistress between 1846 and 1854. She and Flaubert saw each other only very rarely, however, and their liaison existed mainly in their letters. As with so many other things, Flaubert found to his dismay that Louise in the flesh was not the same as Louise in his imagination. As a result, he usually preferred a solitary life at Le Croisset to other pursuits.

Flaubert has often been considered a misanthropic recluse. He was characterized by morbidity and pessimism, which may have been partly due to his illness, and by a violent hatred and contempt for middle-class society, derived ultimately from his childhood in bourgeois Rouen. He was often bitter and unhappy because of the great disparity that existed between his unattainable dreams and fantasies and the realities of his life; for example, his mystical and idealized love for Elisa adversely affected all his later relationships with women. Flaubert's unhappiness and loneliness is perhaps best expressed by his famous remark, "Madame Bovary, c'est moi."

Although Flaubert gained renown as a writer within his own lifetime, he was not financially successful (he made only 500 francs for the first five years' sales of *Madame Bovary*), and he was hurt by the enmity and misunderstanding of his critics and readers. At the height of public hostility, in 1857, he and the publisher of *Madame Bovary* were tried for an "outrage to public morals and religion." However, the case was finally acquitted.

Flaubert's works include *Madame Bovary* (1857); *Salammbo* (1862), a weighty historical novel about the war between Rome and Carthage; *Sentimental Education* (1869), a novel dealing again with the theme of the frustrations of middle-class life and human aspirations; and *The Temptation of Saint Anthony* (1874), a rich and evocative series of religious tableaux. In 1877 he published *Three Tales,* which contains the beautiful short stories, *A Simple Heart, The Legend of Saint Julian Hospitator,* and *Herodias.* These justly famous stories are masterpieces of short fiction and are among his finest and most moving works. Flaubert's play, *The Candidate,* failed after a few performances in 1874, and his last novel, *Bouvard and Pechuhet,* which was unfinished on his death, was published posthumously in 1881.

Flaubert was one of the most important European writers of the 19th century, and in him the French novel reached a high level of development. None of his later works, except the three short stories, ever equaled the artistic and technical quality of his first novel, and it is primarily on *Madame Bovary* that his reputation rests. Flaubert combined a feeling for the ideals of the Romantic era with the objective outlook and scientific principles of Realism to create a novel which has stood as a monument and example to writers ever since.

SUGGESTIONS FOR FURTHER READING

Brereton, Geoffrey. *A Short History of French Literatute.* Baltimore, 1954 (paperback).

Levin, Harry. *The Gates of Horn: A Study of Five French Realists.* New York, 1963.

Spencer, Philip. *Flaubert: A Biography.* New York, 1952.

Steegmuller, Francis. *Flaubert and Madame Bovary: A Double Portrait.* New York, 1957 (paperback).

——————————————, ed. *Selected Letters of Gustave Flaubert,* New York, 1954 (paperback).

Thorlby, Anthony. *Gustave Flaubert and the Art of Realism.* New Haven, 1957.

Turnell, Martin. *The Novel in France*. New York, 1958 (paper-back).

BOOKS BY FLAUBERT AVAILABLE IN PAPERBACK EDITIONS

Madame Bovary   *A Dictionary of Platitudes*
Salammbo   *Sentimental Education*
Three Tales

SAMPLE EXAMINATION QUESTIONS

1. Discuss the attitude of Flaubert towards the middle-class society he is describing. Use illustrations from the novel to support your view.

2. Explain the use of contrast and irony in *Madame Bovary*.

3 Compare the characterizations of Homais and Bournisien. What do they each represent? What is Flaubert's reaction to them? Are they fairly portrayed?

4. In what ways is *Madame Bovary* a realistic novel? What is "realism," in a literary sense?

5. Analyze the personality of Emma Bovary. How is she responsible for her own downfall? How do the nature of provincial society and the people around her make her unhappiness inevitable?

6. Compare Emma's relationships with Charles, Rodolphe, and Leon, in terms of her attitudes and needs, the types of men they are, and the stage of her life during which she meets them.

7. Discuss the use of symbolism in *Madame Bovary,* giving examples from the text.

8. Briefly describe Flaubert's career as a writer and his place in the history of literature.

9. Analyze the personality of Charles Bovary. Why did Emma marry him? Does he contribute to her downfall? Is he a sympathetic character?

10. Identify the following characters: Lagardy, Lariviere, Justin, Felicite, Canivet, Hippolyte, Roualt.

11. Discuss the fantasies that motivate Emma and cause her unhappiness. In what way are they unrealistic? What do they indicate about her personality? Does the kind of problem that Emma suffered from still exist today, and if so, what media cater to the desires of people like her?

12. Analyze the structure of *Madame Bovary* as a novel, pointing out the major scenes, the relationships between incidents and characters, the use of theatrical techniques, and the overall dramatic form.

NOTES

function of Héloïse

Style - delayed emergence
part 1, ch. 6 - portrait of Emma

Charles' lack of imagination,
submission, admiration

romanticism (19)
parallel to us all 24

symbol of bridal bouquet 25

Homais - stereotype 26

clubfoot operation - everybody
thinks of him/herself & not O
their business, not of Hippolyte

NOTES

NOTES

NOTES